REMEMB

PEARL HARBOR

Collectibles

"REMEMBER
PEARL
HARBOR"

Frank B. Arian, M.D.
Martin S. Jacobs

Pictorial Histories Publishing Company Inc.
Missoula, Montana

LIBRARY OF CONGRESS
CONTROL NUMBER 00 135707

ISBN 1-57510-080-0

Second Printing March 2001
Printed in Canada

Layout by Stan Cohen
Typography by Jan Taylor
on Macintosh utilizing:
Aldus Pagemaker 6.5
Adobe Photoshop 5.0

Cover graphics by Egeler Design

Cover Photo: One of the most dramatic photos of World War II is the explosion of the USS Shaw *in the floating dry-dock YFD #2. The* Shaw *was hit by three 250–kg. bombs that were meant for the* Nevada. *One passed through the bridge, igniting fires and rupturing fuel tanks. The blazing oil fires caused the forward magazine to explode in a fiery blast that tore the ship's bow off. The* Nevada *with the tug* Hoga is on the right. USN

PICTORIAL HISTORIES PUBLISHING COMPANY, INC.
713 South Third West, Missoula, Montana 59801
Ph. (406) 549-8488 FAX (406) 728-9280 phpc@montana.com

Photo Credits

USN - United States Navy Archives
FDR - Franklin D. Roosevelt Library, Hyde Park, New York
LC - Library of Congress
HA - Hawaii Archives
PHPC - Pictorial Histories Publishing Company Archives

The Pearl Harbor History Associates, Inc.

This organization was charted as a nonprofit corporation in Virginia in 1985 for the purpose of "education, research and promulgation of historical data" surrounding the events of December 7, 1941, and the War in the Pacific. The Association has produced a copyrighted chart of the ship locations in Pearl Harbor as of 0800 hours on December 7. For information contact:

Ernest Arroyo
Box 1007
Stratford CT 06614
Ph. (203) 378-2353

The Pearl Harbor Survivors Association, Inc.

This organization was established in 1958 as the national group for military personnel who were on or within a three–mile radius of Oahu on December 7, 1941. Reunions are held every two years at different locations and every fifth year on Oahu. For information on the organization, write:

Pearl Harbor Survivors Association, Inc.
Box 99
Menomonee Falls WI 53052-0099
Ph. (262) 251-0787

A sons and daughters association was also established in 1972 to perpetuate the memory of the participants of the attack. For information on the organization, write:

Sons & Daughters of Pearl Harbor Survivors
15752 Caminito Atico
San Diego CA 92128

PSNY 3-7-41 25M
Original
U.(NAVAL AIR STATION, KODIAK ALASKA
NAVAL COMMUNICATIONS

Heading NFC NR 63 F L Z F5L 071830 C8Q TART 0 BT

From: CINCPAC | Date 7 DEC 41

To: ALL SHIPS PRESENT AT HAWAIIN AREA.

Info: - U R G E N T -

DEFERRED unless otherwise checked | ROUTINE........ | PRIORITY........ | AIRMAIL........ | MAILGRAM........

AIRRAID ON REARLHARBOR X THIS IS NO DRILL

07014

RM 58 1910 7DEC

Comdg Off	Exec	Comm	Oper	Supply	Disb	Med'l	Aerog	Pers	Pub Wks	Mar Det	A & R	Files	FAD	NRAB	OOD	WDO	

A–Denotes action   I–Denotes information   X–Denotes copy only

Navy officer Logan C. Ramsey supposedly sent out the famous message "AIR RAID ON PEARL HARBOR X THIS IS NO DRILL." In 1937 he had written an article entitled "Aerial Attacks on Fleets at Anchor." He later commanded the USS *Lake Champlain*.

Introduction

The Memories are as Powerful as the Collectibles

On the morning of December 7, 1941, Honolulu drowsed under the morning dew. The dawn of another tropical Sunday morning served as testament to the natural serenity to which the inhabitants of this island had become accustomed. The temperature was a warm 71 degrees; doves cooed and mynas chattered. The tame Waikiki surf rolled softly onto the white sands of its idyllic deserted beach. Immediately to the west, U.S. naval color guards stood poised in dutiful preparation of hoisting the proud Stars and Stripes above the decks of over 90 ships of the Pacific Fleet stationed at Pearl Harbor.

Just before 8 AM, tranquility was soon disturbed by the distant droning of aircraft engines, emanating from a placid azure sky. Attacking from the north, over majestic saw–toothed mountains and the fields of pineapples and sugar cane, the first of two waves of Japanese fighters, dive bombers and torpedo planes swooped over Pearl Harbor, unleashing a firestorm of abject devastation. Deafening explosions accompanied the acrid odor of sulfur that permeated the smoke–filled air as an idle and vulnerable naval fleet was mercilessly bombarded. Set ablaze by burning pools of oil, the ocean was soon transformed into an inferno, incinerating the trapped young American sailors as they struggled to respond to this overwhelming blitz of Japanese firepower.

As the barrage grew in intensity, singular acts of courage rose above the reigning chaos. Scalded sailors braved the devastation to swim to the rescue of wounded buddies floundering hopelessly amidst wreckage in the harbor. Men plunged fearlessly below decks of smoldering and rapidly sinking ships in heroic efforts to save their entombed fellow crew members. Two vastly outnumbered American aviators, one with wounds to an arm and a leg, joined forces to shoot down eight of 29 Japanese planes to be eliminated in the dogfights that ensued.

Exacting its greatest toll in the first 20 minutes of its two–hour assault, this surprise onslaught from approximately 350 enemy planes succeeded in destroying 162 American aircraft, maiming 16 naval vessels, among them six battleships. Leaving 2,403 Americans dead and 1,178 wounded in its wake, this surprise aggression upon a peaceful nation remains eternally etched into the collective consciousness of our people. Fulfilling the legacy foretold by president Franklin D. Roosevelt, December 7, 1941, became indeed "A day that will live in infamy."

Responding to this treacherous assault, America immediately declared war on Japan and its Axis confederates of Germany and Italy. Intoning a resolute American spirit, the phrase "Remember Pearl Harbor" soon emerged not only to memorialize the events of that historic day but also to serve as a timeless call for collective vigilance and unity. The phrase entered American folklore instantly, and its popularity soon dictated its appearance on a variety of items including posters, banners, music sheets, jewelry, matchbooks, greeting cards, hand bags, magazine ads, stamps and stickers, wall plaques, drinking glasses, license plates, postal covers, war toys, games, comic books, trading cards and more. Not only did the phrase serve as a motivational tool in encouraging volunteerism, the purchase of war bonds, and the conserving of resources, but it also reminded the American people to support those in the military making the genuine sacrifices required of the war effort.

Hundreds of books have chronicled the events of the Pearl Harbor attack, and dozens more will surely follow in preparation for it's 60th anniversary in 2001. *Remember Pearl Harbor Collectibles* is the first book of its kind recognizing and cataloging the Pearl Harbor keepsakes, souvenirs, relics and artifacts which are now a cherished American heritage.

Today, collecting "Remember Pearl Harbor" collectibles is still relatively affordable, although prices have risen consistently in recent times. This book will help you recognize these fascinating icons as well as assist hobbyists via our estimated price/value guide insert in the back of the book. For those of you who duly "Remember Pearl Harbor," we hope you enjoy this book, and that you proudly share it with your family, friends, associates, libraries and schools. The memory of Pearl Harbor and its legacy will only continue to strengthen as we share its honor.

Martin S. Jacobs

Table of Contents

14

The Oregonian

ESTABLISHED BY HENRY L. PITTOCK
An Independent Republican Newspaper

Published Daily, Except Sunday, by The Oregonian Publishing Company, Oregonian Bldg., 537 S. W. Sixth Ave., Portland, Oregon. Telephone AT 2121.

Sole ownership of The Oregonian resides in the H. L. Pittock Family and the Scott Company

CAROLINE P. LEADBETTER, President — PALMER HOYT, Publisher

The Oregonian is a member of the Associated Press. The Associated Press is exclusively entitled to the use for publication of all news dispatches credited to it or not otherwise credited in this paper, and also the local news published herein. All rights of publication of special dispatches herein are also reserved.

National Advertising Offices—Paul Block and Associates, 400 Madison ave., New York city; 919 N. Michigan ave., Chicago; General Motors bldg., Detroit; 1420 Walnut, Philadelphia; Monadnock bldg., San Francisco; Chamber of Commerce bldg., Los Angeles; 1411 Fourth Avenue bldg., Seattle; Little bldg., Boston.

DECEMBER 10, 1941

Remember Pearl Harbor!

The reactions of the American citizen of the Pacific coast to the opening of war with Japan are not different from those of his fellow citizen in another part of the country, except that

First to claim they had coined the battle cry "Remember Pearl Harbor" was the *Portland Oregonian* newspaper. Although dated Dec. 10 on the copy of the editorial page where it first appeared, the paper actually hit the streets at 4:45 p.m. on Dec. 9, 1941.

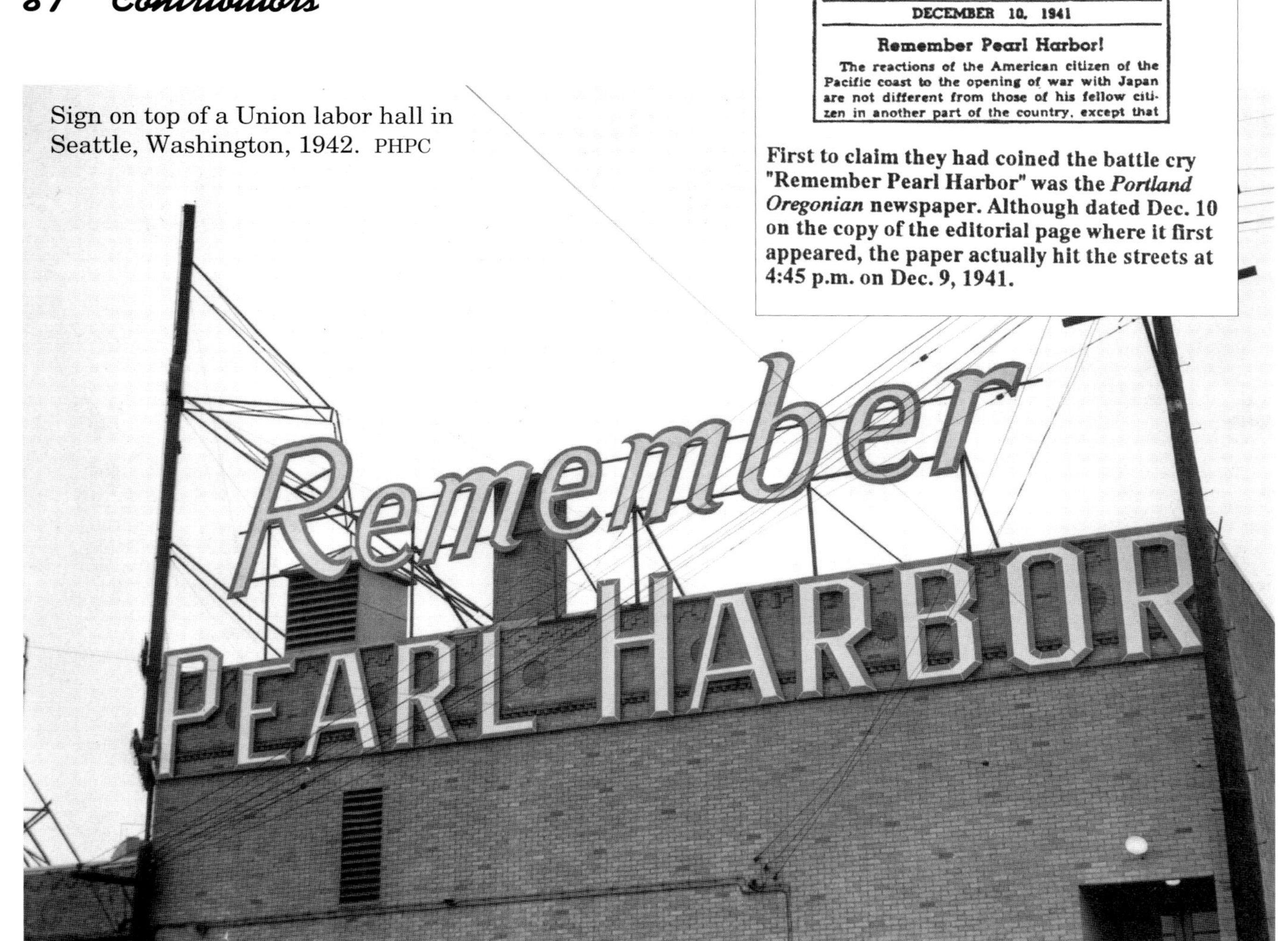

Sign on top of a Union labor hall in Seattle, Washington, 1942. PHPC

The Coming Conflict

GREAT FALLS TRIBUNE

Associated Press — MONTANA'S BEST NEWS GATHERER — United Press

FIFTY-SIXTH YEAR — GREAT FALLS, MONTANA, SUNDAY MORNING, DECEMBER 7, 1941 — PRICE FIVE CENTS

Roosevelt Makes Direct Peace Appeal to Emperor

Coast Guard Takes Over Finn Vessels

Order Issued After Britain Declares War On Little Nation

Cut Bank Man Dies; Driver Faces Arrest

Coroner Demands Trial of Konesky For Auto Deaths

Sparks from the State Wire

Soviets Check Nazi Advances

Japanese Convoys Reported Heading For Gulf of Siam

125,000 Nipponese Stationed In Indo-China Ready to Act

Laboratories At Hamilton Will Expand

Snow at Kalispell

Weather

Nazi Diplomats Map Japan War Aid

The Honolulu Advertiser

Hawaii's Territorial Newspaper

Home Edition

PRICE FIVE CENTS

HONOLULU, HAWAII, U. S. A. FRIDAY MORNING, DECEMBER 5, 1941.

86TH YEAR, NO. 19,764—22 PAGES.

ZERO HOUR NEARS IN PACIFIC; JAPAN REPLIES TO FDR TODAY

War news was at a fever pitch prior to the December 7 attack. The Pacific Fleet had been given a war footing warning as early as November 27.

This June 14, 1941, issue of *Collier's Magazine* had a long article on the defenses of Pearl Harbor. Six months later the Japanese would make a mockery of "Impregnable Pearl Harbor."

These sailors posing on Waikiki Beach would be in for a rude awakening on December 7.

Newspapers

THE RECORD

NO. 28,480 MONDAY, DECEMBER 8, 1941 THREE CENTS

JAPS ATTACK US

350 U.S. Soldiers Killed in Hawaii Raid; Manila Bombed; Batt... Set Afire; Big Sea Fight; Man...

Without the slightest warning, swarms of Japanese bo... day night on the United States.

Sometime before midnight, at least 150 bombers, plainly ... from sea to attack the great American naval base at Pearl ... launched on Manila. Shortly afterward it was reported that ... Late yesterday afternoon, as the attack still continued, Japa...

Washington said 350 soldiers were killed at Pearl Harbo...

There was every indication the Japanese were trying t...

Americans awoke Monday morning to an entirely different world. As one would expect the news was not altogether accurate this early in the reporting.

HEAVY U. S. LOSS

War Pictures Three Full Pages 18, 19 and 20 Others on Pages A, B, C, D, 2, 3, 10, 12

The Philadelphia Inquirer

PUBLIC LEDGER
An Independent Newspaper for All the People

FINAL CITY EDITION

MONDAY MORNING, DECEMBER 8, 1941 THREE CENTS

HAWAII, OUTPOSTS BOMBED; FLEET DESTROYS 4 JAP SUBS

Pearl Harbor Raid Kills 104; 300 Wounded

By FRANCIS McCARTHY

HONOLULU, Dec. 7 (U. P.)—War broke ...

F.D.R. TO TALK TO CONGRESS ON WAR TODAY

President Expected To Ask Declaration In Address to Joint ...

JAPAN STARTS WAR AND THEN ANNOUNCES IT

Declaration Follows Early Meeting of Cabinet; Grew and ...

U. S. Battleship Afire, Second Reported Sunk

By ALEXANDER KENDRICK

Congresswoman Jeannette Rankin of Montana also voted against America's participation in World War I.

Final Edition Closing Market Prices ★★★★

ST. LOUIS STAR-TIMES EXTRA

Vol. 56—No. 59 REISSUE Monday Evening, December 8, 1941 28 Pages Price Three Cents

WAR DECLARED

3,000 Casualties In Jap Attack On Hawaii

Nearly 1,500 Feared Dead

White House Admits Sinking Of One 'Old Battleship' And Destroyer In Pearl Harbor

MANILA, P. I., Dec. 8—(U. P.)—Press dispatches reported that 100 to 200 troops, sixty of them Americans, were killed or injured tonight when Japanese warplanes raided Iba, on the west coast of the Island of Luzon, north of the Olangapo naval base.

WASHINGTON, Dec. 8.—(U. P.)—Casualties on the Hawaiian island of Oahu in yesterday's Japanese air attack will amount to about 3,000, including about 1,500 fatalities, the White House announced today.

The White House confirmed the loss in Pearl Harbor of "one old battleship" and a destroyer, which was blown up.

Several other American ships were damaged and a large number of army and navy airplanes on Hawaiian fields were put out of commission, the White House disclosed.

"We Will Triumph---So Help Us, God"

Congress Acts In 33 Minutes

Jeannette Rankin Only Member Of Either House To Vote 'No' After F. D. R.'s Dramatic Request

WASHINGTON, Dec. 8—(U. P.)—Congressional leaders will take the war resolution to the White House for the President's signature at 2 P. M. today, St. Louis time, the White House announced.

WASHINGTON, Dec. 8.—(U. P.)—Congress today proclaimed existence of a state of war between the United States and the Japanese empire thirty-three minutes after the dramatic moment when President Roosevelt stood before a joint session to pledge that we will triumph—"So help us, God."

The senate acted first, adopting the resolution by a unanimous roll call vote of 82 to 0, within twenty-one minutes after the President had concluded his address to a joint session of both houses.

The house voted immediately afterward and by 1:13 p. m. (12:13 p. m., St. Louis time) a majority of the house had voted "aye."

The final house vote was announced as 388 to 1. The lone ...

Extra **The Charleston Gazette** Extra

The State Newspaper—Associated Press News and Wirephoto

Established 1887. Five Cents. Charleston, West Virginia, Sunday Morning, December 7, 1941. 4 Pages

104 U. S. Troops Killed

Japan Declares

WAR

AmericanMove UpholdsBritish War on Finns

Seizure of 10 to 20 Vessels in Harbors Considered But Prelude to Series Of Economic Restrictions For Aiding Nazis

WASHINGTON, Dec. 6 —(INS)—The U. S. tonight moved swiftly to take over all Finnish flag ships in U. S. ports as an initial measure to endorse Britain's declaration of war against Finland.

City Records Poorly Kept, Audit Shows

Discrepancies, Inefficiency Discovered by State; Law Said Ignored In 16 Instances

Charleston city officials were cited for inefficiencies and fund discrepancies yesterday in a statutory audit which specified 16 instances where the municipality failed to abide by city or state laws.

Lovins Dissents In Mine Ruling

Supreme Court's Majority Narrow and Technical, Jurist Asserts

Fiercer Battles Loom in Libya

More Than 300 Said Wounded On Oahu Isle

Japanese Aircraft Carrier Is Sunk Off Honolulu, Panama Radio Reports; U. S. Battleship Set Afire At Pearl Harbor

Bulletin

WASHINGTON, Dec. 7. — (INS) — The White House announced at 7:45 p. m. EST that preliminary estimates by the war department placed the number of military dead at 104 on the island of Oahu alone.

The number of military wounded was estimated at "more than 300." This report did not place any estimate on civilian casualties.

NEW YORK, Dec. 7.—(INS)—A Japanese aircraft carrier has been sunk off Honolulu, it was stated tonight in a broadcast by the Panama radio picked up by NBC.

TOKYO, Monday, Dec. 8.--(AP)--Japanese headquarters announced at 6 A. M. today that Japan had entered a state of war with the U. S. and Britain in the western Pacific as from dawn today.

NEW YORK, Dec. 7.—(AP)—Japanese warplanes killed 350 men at Hickman field and set fire to the U. S. Battleship Oklahoma today in a sudden raid on Pearl Harbor and Honolulu, an NBC observer radioed direct from the scene today.

Britain Girds To Follow U.S. Into Jap War

Churchill, Winant Confer; Forces In S. Pacific Poised to Assault Nipponese

Cabinet Summoned To Session by FDR

President Expected to Deliver Message to Congress Tomorrow Asking Declaration of War Against Japan After Attack

Jap Planes Bomb Mighty Naval Base

FDR's Note Offered Pledges to Emperor

'Will See This Thing Through' Is American Attitude

Washington Admits Army And Navy Take 'Very Hard Knocks'

Japanese Attempt To Immobilize Fleet And Base Fail

MANDAN DAILY EVENING PIONEER

TODAY'S NEWS TODAY — COMPLETE MARKET REPORT — EVENING EDITION

VOLUME XXVIII—NUMBER 180 PRICE FIVE CENTS MANDAN, NORTH DAKOTA MONDAY EVENING, DECEMBER 8, 1941

U.S. CONGRESS DECLARES WAR

3000 Casualties In Hawaii

One Vote Cast Against War With Japan--Manila Heavily Bombed Today

Terrific Damage Is Reported In Air Raid On Manila — Nichols Airfield Is Target Gasoline Supplies Burning — Guam Is Reported Ablaze

Several Jap Planes And Submarines Destroyed Active Fighting Continues

Battle In Pacific Flames Over Wide Area — Britain Takes Quick Action And Declares War — Losses Reported At Singapore And Hongkong — Thailand Sues For Peace

VETERANS ASK MANDAN TO DISPLAY FLAGS

Japs Claim Two U. S. Battleships Sunk and Many Planes Destroyed

STEWART ASKS GREATER AID TO RED CROSS

14 SHOPPING DAYS to Christmas Also GIVE U.S. Defense Savings BONDS and STAMPS

EXTRA

Los Angeles Times

RACE RESULTS

DAILY, FIVE CENTS

VOL. LXI Three Parts — 38 Pages MONDAY MORNING, DECEMBER 8, 1941. Page A

IT'S WAR!

Hostilities Declared by Japanese; 350 Reported Killed in Hawaii Raid

U.S. Battleships Hit; 7 Die in Honolulu

NEW YORK, Dec. 7. (A.P.)—Three hundred and fifty men were killed by a direct bomb hit on Hickam Field, an N.B.C. observer reported tonight from Honolulu.

In addition to these casualties from an air raid by planes which the observer identified as Japanese, he said three United States ships, including the battleship Oklahoma, were attacked in Pearl Harbor.

Several of the attacking planes, which came from the south, were shot down, he said.

HONOLULU, Dec. 7. (A.P.)—Japanese bombs killed at least seven persons and injured many others, three seriously, in a surprise morning aerial attack on Honolulu today.

Army officials announced that two Japanese planes had been shot down in the Honolulu area.

The dead included three Caucasians, two Japanese and a 10-year-old Portuguese girl.

Several fires were started in the city area, but all were immediately controlled.

Governor Joseph B. Poindexter proclaimed M-Day emergency defense measures immediately in effect. He appointed Eduard Doty in charge of the Major Disaster Council.

The M-Day proclamation establishes civilian-military control of traffic and roads, and permits the Governor to issue food ration regulations.

First reports said that 10 or more persons were injured when enemy planes sprayed bullets on the streets of Wahiawa, a town of about 3000 population, about 20 miles northwest of Honolulu.

This report indicated the aerial attack was aimed at points on the island of Oahu other than Honolulu and the heavily fortified Pearl Harbor naval base.

The attack ended at around 9:25 a.m. (11:55 a.m. P.S.T.)

LATE WAR BULLETINS

SHANGHAI, Dec. 8 (Monday.) (A.P.)—The Japanese have sunk the British gunboat Petrel as it lay off the International Settlement waterfront.

HONOLULU, Dec. 7. (U.P.) — Parachute troops were sighted off Pearl Harbor today.

TOKYO, Dec. 8 (Monday.) (A.P.)—An emergency session of the Japanese Cabinet was held at Premier Tojo's official residence at 7 a.m. today (2 p.m. Sunday, P.S.T.)

NEW YORK, Dec. 7. (U.P.)—The U.S.S. Oklahoma, a battleship, was set afire in today's air attack on Pearl Harbor, an N.B.C. broadcast from Honolulu said.

WASHINGTON, Dec. 7. (A.P.)—The Navy Department announced tonight that a censorship had been placed on all outgoing cablegrams and radio messages from the United States and its outlying possessions.

LONDON, Dec. 7. (#)—The House of Commons was summoned tonight for a session tomorrow.

The House of Lords also was called. An announcement from Prime Minister

Air Guards, Attention!

To chief observers: All observation posts: A.W.S. (Aircraft Warning Service) You are directed to activate your observation posts immediately and to see that the post is fully manned at all times.

By order Brig. Gen. William O. Ryan, Commander, Ft. Interceptor Command.

Air Bombs Rained on Pacific Bases

WASHINGTON, Dec. 7. (A.P.)—The White House announced early tonight that the Navy had advised the President that Japan has attacked the island of Guam.

WASHINGTON, Dec. 7. (A.P.)—Japan declared war upon the United States today. An electrified nation immediately united for a terrific struggle ahead. President Roosevelt was expected to ask Congress for a declaration of war tomorrow.

During the day, Japanese planes bombed Manila, Honolulu, Pearl Harbor, and Hickam Field, Hawaii, without warning. In a broadcast from Honolulu, some 350 soldiers were reported dead at Hickam Field, with numerous casualties at the other points of attack. (The attack on Manila was announced by the White House. The Associated Press correspondent there reported at 1:25 p.m. (P.S.T.) that Manila was quiet.) President Roosevelt said he hoped the report of the bombing of the Philippine capital "at least is erroneous."

Then the Tokyo government announced that Japan had entered a state of war with the United States and Great Britain as of 6 a.m., tomorrow (1 p.m. P.S.T. Sunday.)

But President Roosevelt hardly waited for the Japanese declaration. As soon as he heard of the bombing he ordered the Army and Navy to carry out previously prepared and highly secret plans for the defense of the country.

Army airmen engaged Japanese fighting planes over Honolulu. In the city below them, the White House said, a heavy loss of life had been inflicted, together with extensive damage to property.

At the same time, the Chief Executive called his Cabinet into extraordinary session for 8:30 p.m., and invited Congressional leaders to join the group a half-hour later.

Prior to this meeting, Mr. Roosevelt began the draft of a special message to Congress and if the general sentiment of it would be met in like terms by the Commander-in-Chief.

From a high Congressional source, it was learned that the President had mentioned the possibility of a joint session of Congress tomorrow. This actually led to speculation that the Chief Executive would address it and ask in person, as did Woodrow Wilson in 1917, that it declare war.

EXTRA

TELEPHONE CLASSIFIED ADS TO SUtter 2424 (East Bay, TEmplebar 2424) or bring them to Examiner Office Corner Market and Third Sts

AMERICA FIRST

San Francisco Examiner

Monarch of the Dailies

THE WEATHER Fair and Mild in San Francisco Bay Region Monday

VOL. CLXXV, NO. 161 — SAN FRANCISCO, MONDAY, DECEMBER 8, 1941—28 PAGES — DAILY 5 CENTS, SUNDAY 10 CENTS

U. S.-JAP WAR!

HAWAII, MANILA BOMBED; TWO U. S. WARSHIPS SUNK

BULLETINS

MANILA, Dec. 7.—(INS)—The American ... base at Cavite, Island of Luzon, was sub... to enemy attack this morning. ... Army and Navy authorities commanded ... to their stations to resist the attack. ... were no immediate reports on dam...

HONOLULU, Dec. 7.—(INS)—The ... States Army issued an official state... this morning declaring enemy aircraft ... shot down.

...INGTON, Dec. 7.—(INS)—Senate leaders were ... today for an emergency session tomorrow in an... of a message from President Roosevelt asking ... of war against Japan.

...EDRO, Dec. 7.—(INS)—Every naval officer ... attached to the San Pedro air base was ...

Severe Explosions Rock Pearl Harbor In Surprise Attack

HONOLULU, Dec. 7.—(AP)—Japanese bombs killed at least five persons and injured many others, three seriously, in a surprise morning aerial attack on Honolulu today.

HONOLULU, Dec. 7.—(INS)—America's outpost of the Pacific, mighty Pearl Harbor naval base was under enemy attack today.

A number of attacking planes, with red insignia were sighted shortly after 8 a. m.

Newspaper extra on December 7, 1941, in Redding, California. LC

EXTRA

Spokane Daily Chronicle

56TH YEAR, NO. 67 — 32 PAGES — SPOKANE, WASH., MONDAY, DECEMBER 8, 1941. — PHONE MAIN 1121.

U. S. Weather Report

WAR IS DECLARED ON JAPAN! 3000 CASUALTIES IN HAWAII

WIREPHOTOS RECEIVED TODAY SHOW GUARD OVER VITAL ROADWAY, AND U. S. AIRCRAFT CARRIER REPORTED DAMAGED

Roosevelt Requests Move by Congress

U. S.-Built Bombers Hit Japanese Troop Ships

United States Fleet Hunts Jap Warships

THREE PEOPLE HURT IN CRASH

GERMANS ADMIT MOSCOW'S TOUGH

U. S. AND JAPANESE NAVAL STRENGTH

	U. S.	JAPAN
BATTLESHIPS	17	12
AIRCRAFT CARRIERS	7	8
CRUISERS	37	46
DESTROYERS	170	125
SUBMARINES	113	71
TOTAL	344	262

Farm News
News of interest to farm owners and operators of this section will be found on page 4 of today's Roanoke Times.

THE ROANOKE TIMES

The Weather
VIRGINIA: Increasing cloudiness with rising temperature Monday; Tuesday mostly cloudy and slightly colder.

Vol. CX, No. 161. FULL (AP) ASSOCIATED PRESS SERVICE ROANOKE, VIRGINIA, MONDAY MORNING, DECEMBER 8, 1941. UNITED PRESS SERVICE 14 PAGES. 3 CENTS DAILY 10 CENTS SUNDAY

JAPS OPEN WAR ON U. S.

Roosevelt To Send Special Message To Congress Today As Reports Tell Of Heavy Casualties To Army And Navy

Cabinet Holds Night Meeting With President

Whether This Country Is to Follow Nipponese in Formally Declaring War Uncertain; Foes of President's Foreign Policy Unite in Solid Front

WASHINGTON REMAINS CALM

By RICHARD L. TURNER

WASHINGTON, Dec. 8 (Monday) (AP).—Bombs from Japan made war on the United States today and as death tolls mounted President Roosevelt announced he would deliver in person today a special message to congress...

Sailors Board Bus Here for Home Base

Hawaii, Philippines, Guam Hit Without Warning; Americans Strike Back

Nipponese Include Britain in War Declaration After Planes Spread Terrific Death and Destruction in Honolulu and Pearl Harbor—Claim Two American Battleships Sunk in Engagements

SINGAPORE AND EAST INDIES ATTACKED

By THE ASSOCIATED PRESS

Japan assaulted every main United States and British possession in the central and western Pacific and invaded Thailand today (Monday) in a hasty but evidently shrewdly-planned prosecution of a war she began Sunday without warning.

Her formal declaration of war against both the United States and Britain came two hours and 55 minutes after Japanese planes spread death and terrific destruction in Honolulu and Pearl Harbor at 7:35 a. m., Hawaiian time (1:05 p. m. EST) Sunday.

The claimed successes for this fell swoop included sinking ... U. S. Battleship West Virginia and setting afire ...

THE MUSKEGON CHRONICLE

Muskegon "The Port City"

Muskegon, Michigan, Monday, December 8, 1941 Twenty Pages—Three Cents

Two American Warships Are Sunk by Japanese Forces

CONGRESS DECLARES WAR

US Forces Lose 3,000 Dead, Wounded

Tokyo Reports Big Damage To American Naval Vessels

Reported Set Afire

Late Bulletins

Says Curse of World Rests On Roosevelt

House and Senate Cheer President's Call for Conflict

Rush for Chronicle Extras Sell 13,000 in W. Michigan

Japanese Warned Of Long Conflict

Defense Housing Project Built Here Is Investigated

Mercury Drops, Snow Flurries Are Due Tuesday

Goodfellow Christmas Fund

"Let No Child Be Forgotten"

G. R. Soldier Is Killed in Action

Where to Find It

WAR EXTRA! WAR EXTRA!

Seattle Post-Intelligencer

SEATTLE, MONDAY, DECEMBER 8, 1941

TWENTY PAGES DAILY 5c, SUNDAY 10c

JAPAN, U. S. AT WAR

104 DIE IN HAWAII RAID; 2 U. S. TRANSPORTS SUNK

All Military Posts In Seattle Region Go on War Basis

BRITAIN GETS READY FOR WAR AGAINST JAPS

Two American Warships Lost In Pearl Harbor

TOKYO SAYS AT LEAST ONE AIR CARRIER USED

President Drafting Special Message; Cabinet in Session

New Warning On Planes

War Map

TODAY'S

WAR BULLETINS

Guam Naval Base Also Attacked During Morning

Come and get $100 MORE for Your Car ... in trade on a New 1942 HUDSON. 30,000 MILE GUARANTEE PLAN. EASY TERMS! SEE DICK DUBOIS

Honolulu Star-Bulletin 2nd EXTRA

8 PAGES—HONOLULU, TERRITORY OF HAWAII, U. S. A., SUNDAY, DECEMBER 7, 1941—8 PAGES

PRICE FIVE CENTS

DEATHS OVER 400 ON OAHU, LATEST REPORT

TOKYO ANNOUNCES "STATE OF WAR" WITH U. S.

Japanese Raids On Guam, Panama Are Reported

Oahu Blackout Tonight; Fleet Here Moves Out to Sea

Four Waves, Start At 7:55, Oahu Hit In Many Places

BULLETIN

Honolulu and Oahu came through a baptism of fire today with calm and determination as wave after wave of Japanese bombers rained missiles all over the island.

At 3 this afternoon army, navy, the police and various civilian agencies were on a war footing, and faced possible further attacks with undaunted vigor and courage.

At 3 p. m. the police reported that, based on information from the city emergency hospital and the morgue there are 25 known dead and 56 known injured in the bombing raids.

In Washington President Roosevelt announced that the raids were by Japanese bombers.

A United Press dispatch at 3 this afternoon said that estimates given out at Washington are that 400 are dead and 300 injured of the army forces on Oahu alone.

Japanese raiding planes struck hardest at the army and navy bases, but the city of Honolulu itself suffered severe damage.

Deaths on Oahu are reported at more than 400, counting army and civilian fatalities. Navy casualties have not been announced.

Estimate of the army deaths was given out in a White House statement at Washington tonight.

REPORTS GUAM, PANAMA ATTACKED

Unconfirmed reports this afternoon based on fragmentary broadcast reports heard on mainland stations, were that both Guam and Panama had been attacked by the Japanese.

Press association dispatches mentioned possible attacks on Manila but there was no confirmation of this.

WASHINGTON, Dec. 7. (U.P.)—The White House tonight issued a preliminary estimate that 400 were dead and more than 300 wounded in the army forces alone on Oahu. Civilian casualties were not mentioned.

NEW YORK, Dec. 7. (U.P.)—NBC tonight heard the Panama radio broadcast that a Japanese aircraft carrier was sunk off Honolulu.

SHANGHAI, Monday, Dec. 8. (U.P.)—The Osaka Mainichi reported from Tokyo today that Japanese imperial headquarters announced a naval battle between the Japanese and the British and American fleets is going

Continued on Page 3, Col. 3

Governor Proclaims National Emergency

"I do declare and proclaim a defense period to exist throughout the territory of Hawaii.

This hereby puts the M-Day bill into full effect.

Known Oahu Casualties

BOMB DAMAGE: The interior of the ... home at Liliha and Kuakini Sts., hit by a bomb.

WASHINGTON PLACE BOMB.

BULLETINS

By THE UNITED PRESS

WASHINGTON, Dec. 7.—The White House announced tonight it feared there was heavy loss of life in Hawaii.

NEW YORK, Dec. 7.—The National Broadcasting Co. tonight reported 350 men killed in a direct hit on Hickam field, the army's giant air field on Oahu.

NEW YORK, Dec. 7.—NBC reported from Honolulu tonight that the battleship Oklahoma was set afire during the Pearl Harbor attack.

Military Censorship On All Messages

Blackout For Oahu Ordered

Inter-Island Ships, Planes Are Held Up

Two Japanese Fliers Captured

Editorial

HAWAII MEETS THE CRISIS

THE NASHVILLE TENNESSEAN

In the Inner Citadel of the Nation

NASHVILLE, TENN., THURSDAY MORNING, DECEMBER 18, 1941

3 RANKING NAVAL, ARMY OFFICERS IN HAWAII AREA LOSE COMMANDS

House Gets New Bill, Urgent Plea on Douglas Dam

Japanese Pincer Attempt in Malaya

American Units Blast Japs Who Push Singapore

Drastic Shakeup Comes as Board Launches Probe

Kimmel Replaced as Fleet Chief By Nimitz; Heads of Army's Land And Air Corps on Island Ousted

Mayor To Fight For Bond Vote

Bandits Get $90 Off Bus Driver

Rebellious House Beats Efforts For Draft Limit Below 21 Years

Tire Rationing Begins Jan. 4

Sergeant York Says:—

Gallant Hong Kong Hold; Spurn Surrender

The Traffic Toll

Emergency War Relief Drive For $200,000 Here Opens Today

German Retreat From Moscow Too Fast To Bury Dead, Says Witness; Frozen Bodies Dot Roads

Cost of Living Reported Higher

The San Francisco News

WAR SUNSET FINAL EXTRA

NEW CAL. SUB RAIDS JAPS ON WAKE

1 Tanker Sunk; 1 Reaches Port

Late Bulletins

ISLE SEIZURE FROM MARINES IS CLAIMED

OLD GLORY FLIES ON

LIFEBOATS ARE FIRED ON, SAY U.S. SURVIVORS

Churchill at F. R. Parley Tells Grand Strategy Need

3 TROOPSHIPS SUNK AT LUZON

Vast Allied War Program Expected in Epochal Meet

INDUSTRY PACT WITH LABOR

S. F. WARNED OF FLAGRANT HOARDING

Hongkong Springs Trap

War Summary

WELDERS ASK NAVY TO RUN SHIPYARDS

BRITISH SINK SIX MORE AXIS SHIPS

Italy General Killed

FRIDAY—WAR MAPS!

WHICH IS GREATER THREAT TO U. S.—GERMANY OR JAPAN? SEE RESULTS OF GALLUP POLL, PAGE 8

SABOTEURS LAND HERE!

Britain, Australia Declare War!

The Honolulu Advertiser

HONOLULU, HAWAII, U.S.A., MONDAY MORNING, DECEMBER 8, 1941

RAIDERS RETURN IN DAWN ATTACK

Carnage in King Street

Advertiser Men Watch Grim Show

Boil Water! During Test

FLASH BULLETINS

Civilian Toll 37 Dead, Many Hurt

Enjoy Carefree HOLIDAYS! FIRESTONE CHAMPIONS

THE VON HAMM-YOUNG CO., LTD.

One of the great controversies of World War II was the replacement of Admiral Husband Kimmel, General Walter Short and General Frederick Martin as head of the US Navy, US Army and US Army Air Forces in Hawaii. They were accused of the supposed unpreparedness of United States Forces in Hawaii prior to the attack and to this day have not been totally vindicated of these accusations.

As one can tell from these headlines in the Honolulu and San Francisco newspapers, the Pearl Harbor attack produced much confusion and hysteria in Hawaii and on the West Coast of the United States. The Japanese did not attack Hawaii again after the second wave on December 7, although in March 1942 an enemy submarine did launch a seaplane which overflew Oahu and dropped several bombs which did no damage. There were a number of Japanese submarine attacks on American shipping between Hawaii and California in late 1941 and 1942. The island of Wake, 1,500 miles west of Hawaii, was captured by Japanese forces on December 24, 1941, after a heroic 16–day battle by US Marines and civilian contractors.

Decals & Patches

Sticker

Windows all over America were plastered with decals and stickers reminding the nation not to forget the attack on Pearl Harbor.

Decal

This remarkable photo, taken in the midst of the second wave, shows the concentrated antiaircraft fire the attacking planes had to fly through. The *Nevada* had sortied as had the *Neosho* and *Vestal*, which times this photo about 0900. The photo was taken from the Koolau Mountains at the corner of Puliki Place and Aiea Heights Drive. USN

Badge

Design also used as a decal of the class coat of arms for the Army Air Forces Basic Flying School at Moffett Field, California, January 1942. It needs no explanation.

Sticker

Patches

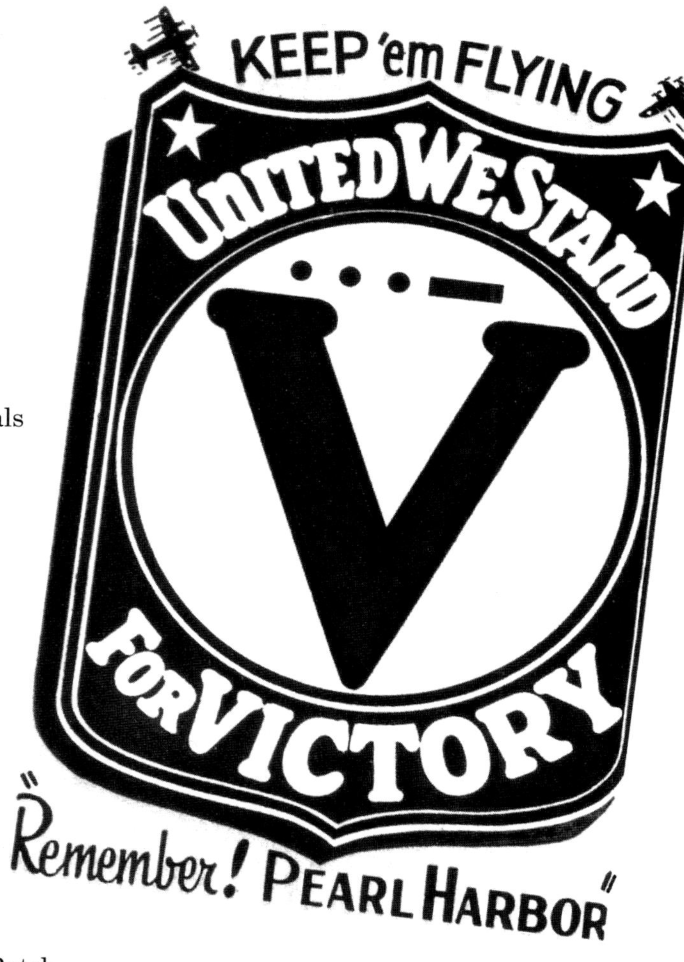

Decals

Patch

REMEMBER PEARL HARBOR | REMEMBER PEARL HARBOR | REMEMBER PEARL HARBOR | REMEMBER PEARL HARBOR

REMEMBER PEARL HARBOR | REMEMBER PEARL HARBOR | REMEMBER PEARL HARBOR | REMEMBER PEARL HARBOR

Badge inserts

Patches

Decal

View of the Marine barracks' parade grounds at the Navy yard between 0930 and 1030. The skies have been darkened by billowing clouds of black smoke from the crippled ships of battleship row. USN

Post Cards, Bubble Gum Cards, Cinderellas & Matchbooks

Post cards were another important means to remind all Americans what they were fighting for.

Bubble gum cards appealed to kids before and during the war, just as they do today. Gum Inc. of Philadelphia, with its "Blong" gum, put out hundreds of different scenes on their cards from 1939 on through the war. The attack on Pearl Harbor, of course, would be one of the greatest wartime events to appear on the cards.

Sticker

These "Heroes of Pearl Harbor" cards were a series of eight, red with white accents, that were printed on the front and back panels of a candy box, manufactured by Candyland Co. of Brooklyn, New York.

1

REMEMBER
PEARL
HARBOR
•• December 7th, 1941 ••

2

WE WANT PEACE
REMEMBER PEARL HARBOR!
COPYRIGHT H·A·BRAND CINCINNATI, O.
THE PEACE THEY GAVE US

3

REMEMBER
PEARL
HARBOR
DEC. 7th, 1941

4

5

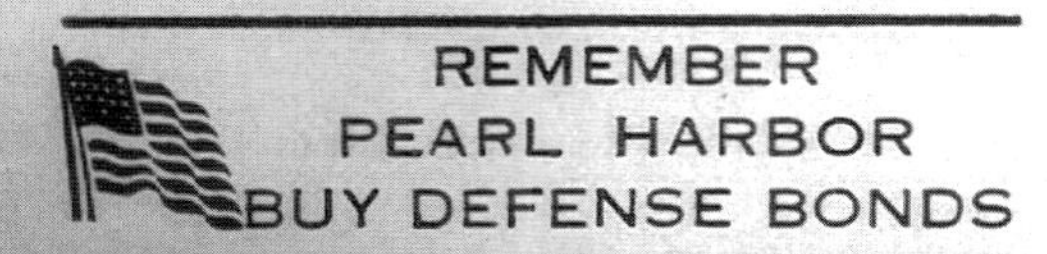

6

REMEMBER
PEARL
HARBOR
V
DEC. 7th
1941

7

8

Remember Pearl Harbor
& Sacrifice For Defense

9

10

11

REMEMBER
PEARL HARBOR
AND BUY DEFENSE BONDS

Assorted stickers

1

2

3

4

5

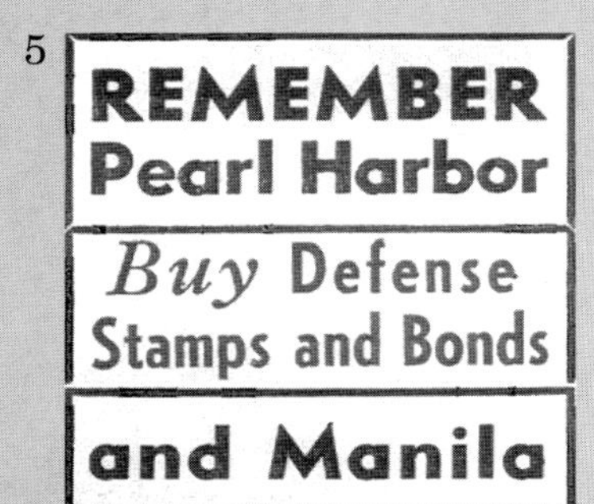

6

7

8

Cinderellas are small poster–like stickers which were used extensively during the war, usually on letters or packages to remind American citizens to keep up their resolve to defeat the enemy.

9

10

11

AIRCRAFT
REMEMBER PEARL HARBOR!

1
REMEMBER PEARL HARBOR
Help the Boys in Service Exterminate These Rats—Buy War Bonds & Stamps!
Post cards
2
THE THREE DIRTY DOGS
REMEMBER PEARL HARBOR
3
HELP
Win the War...
Defeat the Axis
FOR VICTORY
BUY
BONDS
STAMPS
(Over)
REMEMBER PEARL HARBOR
REMEMBER
PEARL HARBOR
4
REMEMBER PEARL HARBOR
W.G.N. FLAG & DEC. CO. CHI.
5
6
"REMEMBER PEARL HARBOR"
7
REMEMBER PEARL HARBOR
8
Remember
PEARL
HARBOR
9
REMEMBER
PEARL HARBOR
13
Remember Pearl Harbor
V FOR VICTORY
Buy Defense Stamps and Bonds
Pillsbury's Best Flour
10
Remember Pearl Harbor
11
BUY DEFENSE BONDS
REMEMBER PEARL HARBOR!
12
REMEMBER PEARL HARBOR!

HEROES OF PEARL HARBOR
KILLED IN ACTION
Captain Colin Kelly Jr.
who sank the Haruna

1

Colin Kelly was America's first hero of the war but not the way he was portrayed during and for many years after the war. Kelly was the pilot of a B-17 bomber that supposedly dropped three bombs on the Japanese battleship *Haruna* on December 10, 1941, in the Philippines. His bomber was then shot up by Japanese fighters, and he ordered his crew to bail out before crash–landing. He did not survive. For this action he was posthumously awarded the Distinguished Service Cross. Kelly was even reported to have flown his plane "down the funnels of the *Haruna,*" which was totally false. Kelly's plane did bomb a Japanese cruiser, the *Ashigara,* but did not sink her. America needed a quick hero after the disastrous Pearl Harbor and Philippines attacks, and Kelly was a perfect candidate—West Point graduate, pilot who saved his crew and supposedly heroically crash–landed into an enemy battleship.

2

DISPLAY THE COLORS

THIS BOOK CONTAINS 50 STAMPS

For use on all stationery, envelopes, post cards packages, etc.

Price 50 Cents

Name of Your Organization Imprinted Here

REMEMBER PEARL HARBOR

USA

3

4

REMEMBER PEARL HARBOR

5

6

7

8

9

10

1

2

3

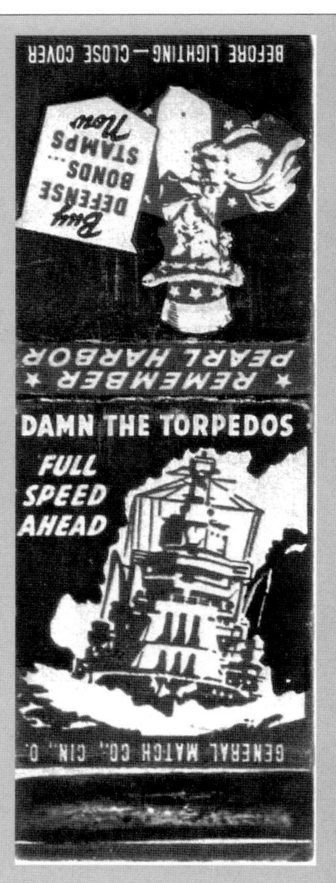

4

5

6

7

Matchbooks were another printed item that promoted the war effort, both at home and overseas.

Posters, Pennants & Banners

Poster

DECEMBER 7th

Remember Pearl Harbor

WORK-FIGHT-SACRIFICE

Let Every American
Remember the Destruction at
Pearl Harbor, Hawaii
Sunday, Dec. 7, 1941
Keep 'em Flying
Until Peace is Restored
Throughout the World.
America and Freedom.

Sticker

Window sign

Poster

Banner

We have just begun to fight!

PEARL HARBOR
BATAAN
CORAL SEA
MIDWAY
GUADALCANAL
NEW GUINEA
BISMARCK SEA
CASABLANCA
ALGIERS
TUNISIA

Poster

Sign

Stickers

BUY STAMPS AND BONDS

WE WILL
WIN THIS
WAR
WITH YOUR
HELP AND
THE HELP
OF EVERY
AMERICAN
LET'S GO
REMEMBER
PEARL
HARBOR

SACRIFICE FOR DEFENSE

Sticker

Assorted pennants

Banners

The remains of a B-17C rest on the tarmac near Hangar 5 at Hickam Field on December 7. USN

Remember PEARL Harbor
OF
FREEDOM
KEEP 'EM ROLLING
KEEP 'EM FLYING
REMEMBER PEARL HARBOR
ON TO VICTORY

Banners

PEARL
HARBOR

Remember
PEARL HARBOR

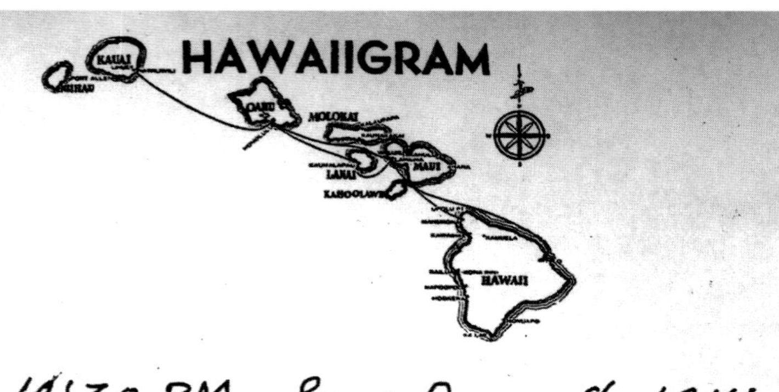

10:30 P.M. Sun. June 8, 1941

HAWAII -- the Land of Scenery, Sunshine & Gaiety

Lois Honey:

There was a report of an actual attempt of sabotage on this island of Oahu. The U.S. Army Air Corp has bombers flying over the Island every day with loaded bomb racks. We have patrols on the hi-ways. We have a ½ ton army truck with a mounted machine gun, and two rifle grenadiers with fixed bayonets.

I am sending you a picture of me which I had taken on maneuvers last month. Another soldier and I were on guard when this was taken. We were armed with rifle and pistol and carried real bullets. We were guarding the Communications supplies. I haven't had any sleep for 72 hours.

Well until next time, I still am,

Affectionately
Lo Elmer [illegible]

P.S. Please answer soon and send picture.

Letters & Postal Covers

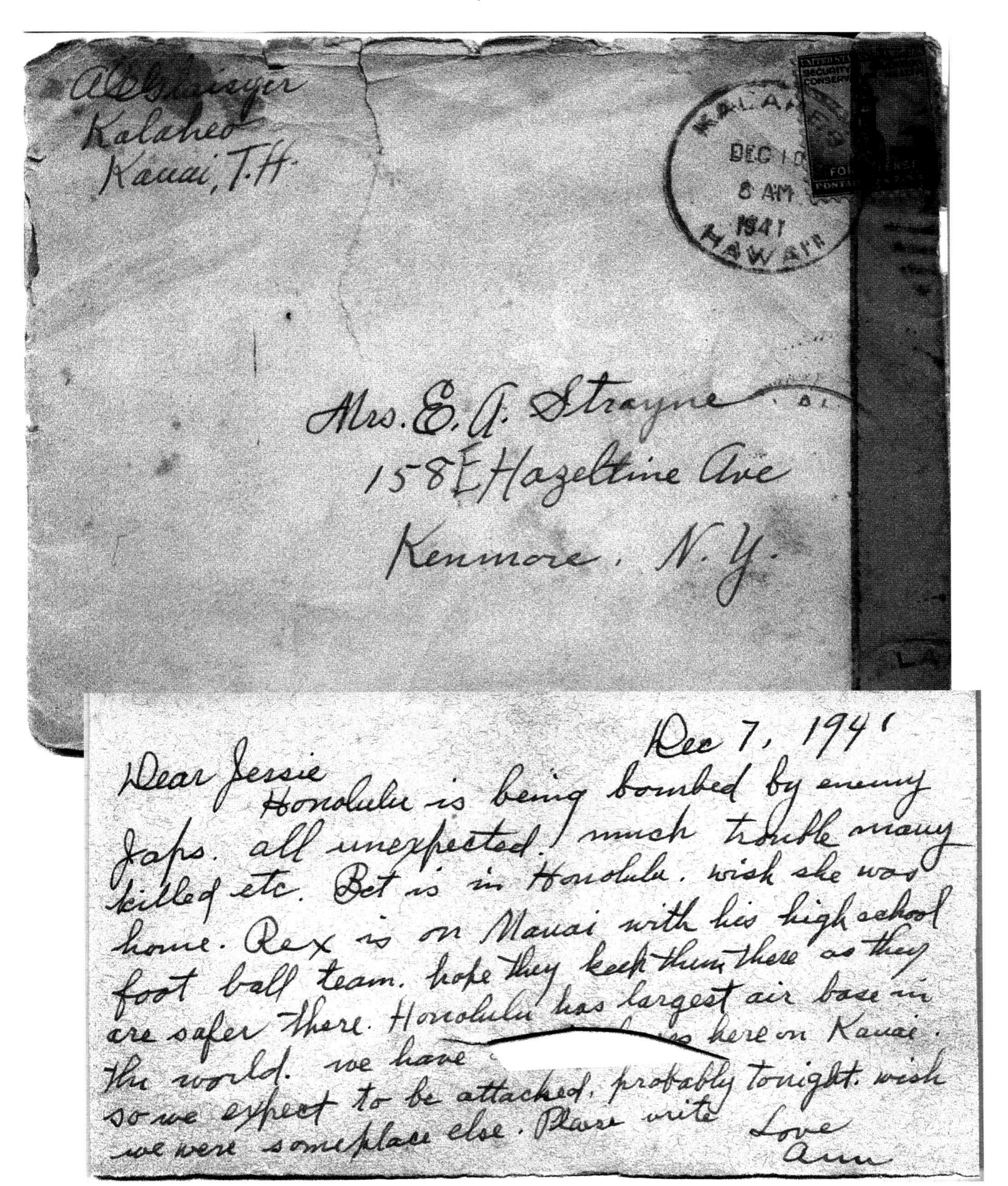
Al Grainger
Kalaheo
Kauai, T.H.

Mrs. E. A. Strayne
158 E Hazeltine Ave
Kenmore, N.Y.

Dec 7, 1941

Dear Jessie
Honolulu is being bombed by enemy Japs. all unexpected! much trouble many killed etc. Bet is in Honolulu. wish she was home. Rex is on Maui with his high school foot ball team. hope they keep them there as they are safer there. Honolulu has largest air base in the world. we have [cut out] here on Kauai. so we expect to be attacked, probably tonight. wish we were someplace else. Please write

Love
Ann

Censorship was in place immediately after Pearl Harbor and lasted throughout the war. This letter was written on December 7 and mailed to the mainland on the 10th. Notice the cut–out in the letter.

Monday Morning
12, January, 1942

Good Morning my Very own Dearest Madeline:-
Just a few lines then Will get this on its Way.
This sure is some Stationary, could use more
of this if you could get it Without to much bother.
It has caused a lot of Comments on the Ship.
Got turned in last night at 1015 P.M and up at
6 15 A.M this morning.
Weather is Sunshiny and much warmer.
Thanks again for all the Christmas presents,
Cards and New Years Cards.
a Hello to all the Folks.
Hope making out the Defense Bonds isn't too
much bother.
Remember keep that "Smile Smiling".
To the Bestest Sweetheart anyone ever Had

Lovingly, your Very own
John.
(I Love you)

December 7, 1941

Tonight - at 6 oc P.M.
I sit here by lantern
light inside the
telephone exchange.
Today - will go down
in history. I am
alone. ~~My~~ men
have gone to the
fields anywhere to
get away. The place
has been bombed
terribly. We were
caught completely
by surprise. Our
planes were 60%
burned.
This barracks

Dec. 7 41. I was on the
battle ship West Virigina; we got hit
pretty hard - two bombs hit our ship;
that one blew me and a lot of others
over the side. It killed 7 sailors.
I was luckey just my leg & shoulder
broken.

Good luck Morty
and take care
G. R. Williams
Kyle Texas

WORLDS GREATEST NAVY

U. S. S. ARIZONA

BATTLE SHIP NO. 39

NAMED IN HONOR OF
STATE OF ARIZONA

EVER WATCHFUL & ALERT

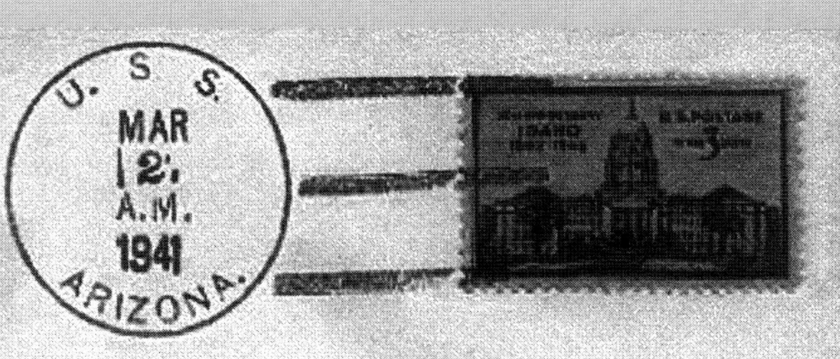

WILLIAM R. WELCH,
2124 31st Ave. So.
Seattle, Washington

The *Arizona* was built at the New York Navy Yard and commissioned October 17, 1916. On the fateful morning of December 7, she was hit by two 800–kg armor piercing bombs dropped by horizontal bombers from the carriers *Kaga* and *Hiryu*. One bomb, at about 0810, penetrated the *Arizona's* forward magazine and in a tremendous blast virtually destroyed the ship with the tragic loss of 1,177 men.

WILLIAM S. LINTO
4920 N. E. 16th AVE.
PORTLAND 11, OREGON

THIS SIDE OF C

REMEMBER
Pearl Harbor
Buy Defense
Stamps and Bonds
and Manila

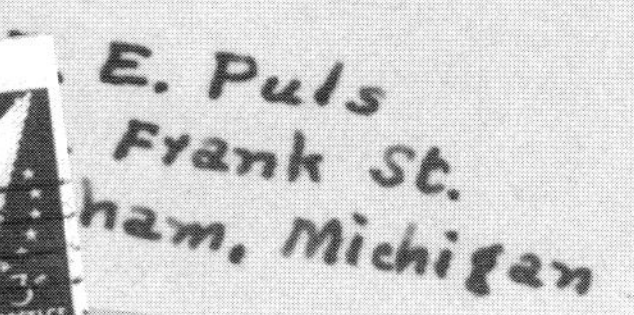

E. Puls
Frank St.
ham, Michigan

DEAD JAPS CAN FIGHT NO MORE!
DEAD JAPS CAN TORTURE NO MORE!
When the little yellow dogs plead for an "honorable and just" peace . . .
REMEMBER:
Pearl Harbor
Bataan
The March of Death
The Jap twisted mentality . . .
REMEMBER! REMEMBER
So Sorry! PLEASE!
NO MERCY!
"Vengeance is Mine, sayeth the Lord!"
'Let's make it a tough, vengeful and uncompromising peace'
THE ANTI-PACIFIST PROPAGANDA COMMITTEE
1666 Court Place Denver 2, Colorado

LOS ANGELES
JUL 8
11 PM
1944
CALIF.

Mr. Arthur Knoll,
660 Emerson Ave.,
Hamilton, Ohio.

Assorted postal covers

NAVY DEPARTMENT
Commandant's Office

PENALTY FOR PRIVATE USE TO AVOID PAYMENT OF POSTAGE

WAR BONDS
New York, N. Y.

COMMEMORATING THE PRINCIPLES OF
"THE UNITED NATIONS"
FIRST DAY COVER
"Remember Pearl Harbor"
And Do Not Forget Wake,
Guam, Midway and Manila
Watchdogs of Our Coastline— They Never Sleep
WASHINGTON JAN 14 9-AM 1943 D.C.
—FIRST DAY OF ISSUE—
JAMES C. MOUBRAY
4218 NICHOLSON ST.
HYATTSVILLE, MD.
Buy YOUR Liberty With Victory Bonds
BUY U. S. WAR BONDS
remember PEARL HARBOR
SUNDAY DECEMBER 7, 1941
"Remember Pearl Harbor"
And Do Not Forget Wake,
LET'S GO! U.S.A. KEEP 'EM FLYING!
Guam, Midway and Manila
UNITED STATES OF AMERICA
Richard Lee Wolf
325 Lindenwood Ave.,
Akron, 1, Ohio

Remember Pearl Harbor
BUY WAR STAMPS AND BONDS
LET'S GO! U.S.A. KEEP 'EM FLYING!
All For One
One For All
DAYTON JUN 7 11 AM 1943 OHIO
VIA AIR MAIL.
Mrs. A. Myers Bagley
P.O. Box 306
Chattanooga, Tennessee
WESTFIELD, MASS. NOV 1 9:30 AM 1944
CENTENARY OF THE TELEGRAPH
UNITED STATES POSTAGE
REMEMBER
PEARL HARBOR
BUY DEFENSE BONDS
GOD BLESS AMERICA
HERBERT R. THORPE
WESTFIELD, MASS.
© 1943 JOHN D. STANARD, ATLANTA, GA.
Remember
LET'S GO! U.S.A. KEEP 'EM FLYING!
Pearl Harbor
GOD BLESS AMERICA
OLD GLORY JUN 14 A.M. 1945 TEX.
Mrs. Walter Jacquay
116 Powler St.
New Haven, Ind.

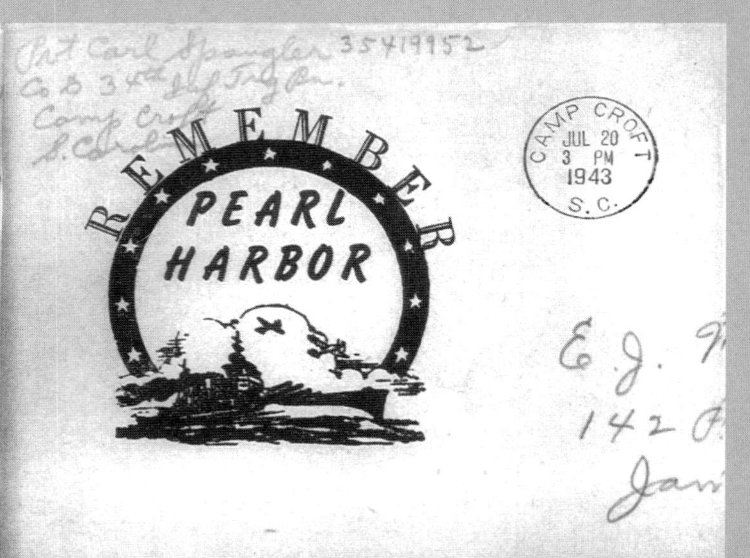

"Remember Pearl Harbor"

And Do Not Forget Wake, Guam, Midway and Manila

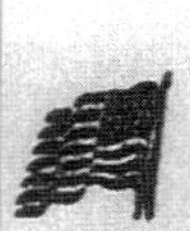

LET'S GO!
☆☆U.S.A.☆☆

H.R. The
Box 444
Westfiel

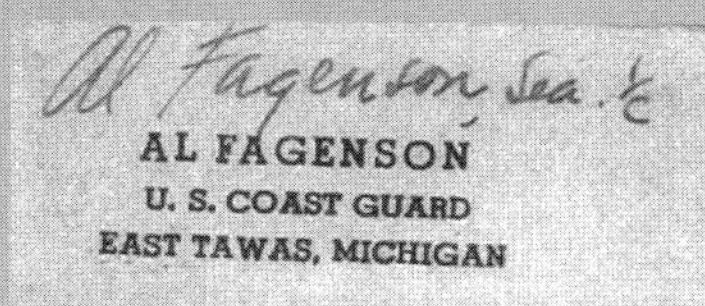

Victor K.
543 N. M
Butl

☆ WORK FOR VICTORY ☆

December 7, 1941

On that Sunday morning Japanese bombers appeared over Pearl Harbor and sank or damaged a number of ships. These attacks brought Japan and the United States into World War II.

Remember Pearl Harbor!

For National Defense

BUY U.S. WAR BONDS

Remember Pearl Harbor

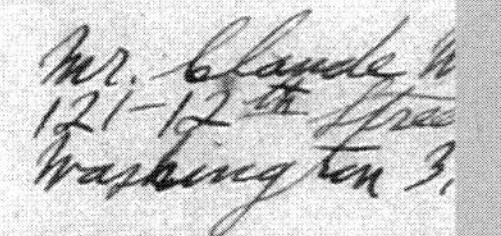

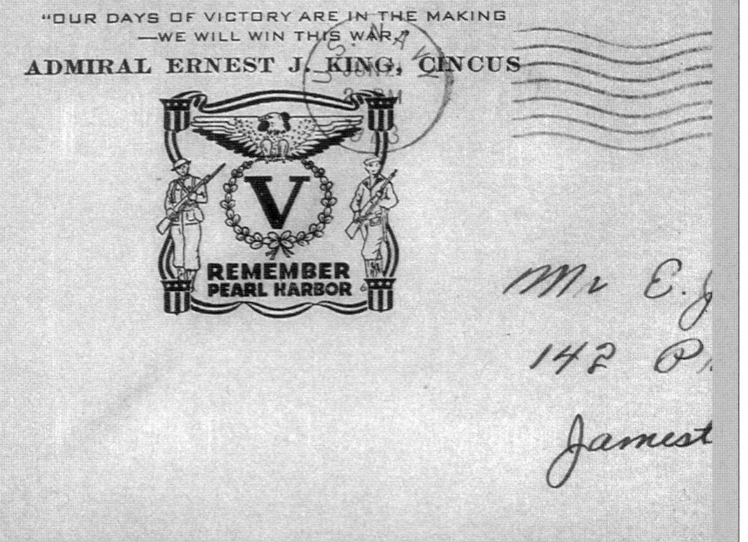

Admiral King (1878-1956) was the overall commander of U.S. Naval operations in World War II and held the dual posts of Chief of Naval Operations and Commander–In–Chief of the U.S. Fleet.

REMEMBER PEARL HARBOR
LAUNCHED For Victory
V
U.S.S.NELSON
SHIPS FOR VICTORY
FOR VICTORY
BUY UNITED STATES WAR BONDS AND STAMPS
Remember
PEARL HARBOR
RICHARD P. BOONE
516 QUEEN STREET
WILMINGTON, NORTH CAROLINA
REMEMBER
PEARL HARBOR
BUY WAR BONDS
"Thunder on! Stride on, Democracy!
Strike with vengeful stroke!"
Walt Whitman.
V
PEARL HARBOR
CORAL SEA
GUADALCANAL
NEW GUINEA
BISMARK SEA
CASABLANCA
BATAAN
MIDWAY
ALGIERS
TUNISIA
KISKA
SALERNO
ROME BERLIN TOKYO

Belles-lettres—P. O. Box 5416, Chi., Ill. Pat. Applied For A. F. Grymes.
Remember—
PEARL HARBOR
Copyright by Thomas Kirksey—© T. K. 1941

Cleveland Cover Club
FIFTH ANNUAL EXHIBITION
VICTORY
REMEMBER
PEARL HARBOR!
entral Y. M. C. A.
Cleveland, O.
May 1—2, 1943

YOUR A SAP, MISTER JAP.
WE WILL AVENGE PEARL HARBOR!
CLEVELAND, OHIO APR 16 1-PM 1942
MICHAEL KOSKO, Jr.
MAHOMET DEC 7 8 AM 1943 ILL.
SECOND ANNIVERSARY OF PEARL HARBOR
REMEMBER PEARL HARBOR
American-Hawaiian Steamship Company
San Francisco, California
HONOLULU HAWAII DEC 7 7:30AM 1942
Richard Stallard, Jr.
3724 Randolph Avenue
Oakland, California
U.S. CENSORS EXAMINED
Commemorating the first anniversary of the treacherous attack on Pearl Harbor by the Japs, December 7, 1941. The first soldier reported killed was Robert Niedzwiecki, (above).
GREENHURST DEC 7 1 PM 1944 N.Y.
DEC. 7 1944
Remember Pearl Harbor
A DATE TO REMEMBER:
A BLACK DAY FOR AMERICA!
WILMINGTON DEC 7 1943 N.C.
Sunday, December 7th, 1941, the Japs attacked—without warning — Pearl Harbor, killing many and sinking several American battleships and destroyers. We, Americans, have a score to settle with Tojo and his cowardly rascals. The day is coming when our boys will march down the streets of Tokyo in glorious victory and until that day all of us must put our support where it will do the most to help. We're Coming Tojo—Soon
DECEMBER 7 1941
BUY MORE WAR BONDS AND STAMPS
VIA AIR MAIL
U.S. DECLARES WAR ON JAPAN!
REMEMBER PEARL HARBOR
ARMY AND NAVY
FOR DEFENSE

CHICAGO BINDER & FILE CO.
720 So. Dearborn Street
CHICAGO, ILLINOIS
REMEMBER PEARL HARBOR
CHICAGO JUN 23 '43 ILL.
U.S. POSTAGE
AMOUNT
.02
PAID
P.B. METER 89214
JAN 24 3 PM 1942 ILL.
UNITED STATES OF AMERICA
INDUSTRY AGRICULTURE
ARMY AND NAVY
SECURITY EDUCATION CONSERVATION HEALTH
FOR DEFENSE
REMEMBER PEARL HARBOR
OPENING DAY
THE MIGHTY 7th WAR LOAN
DRIVE
KENVIL MAY 14 11 AM 1945 N.J.
UNITED STATES POSTAGE
BENJAMIN FRANKLIN
1/2 CENT 1/2
WAR BONDS
J. W. Trevor
Trinity Church
Halifax, N.S.

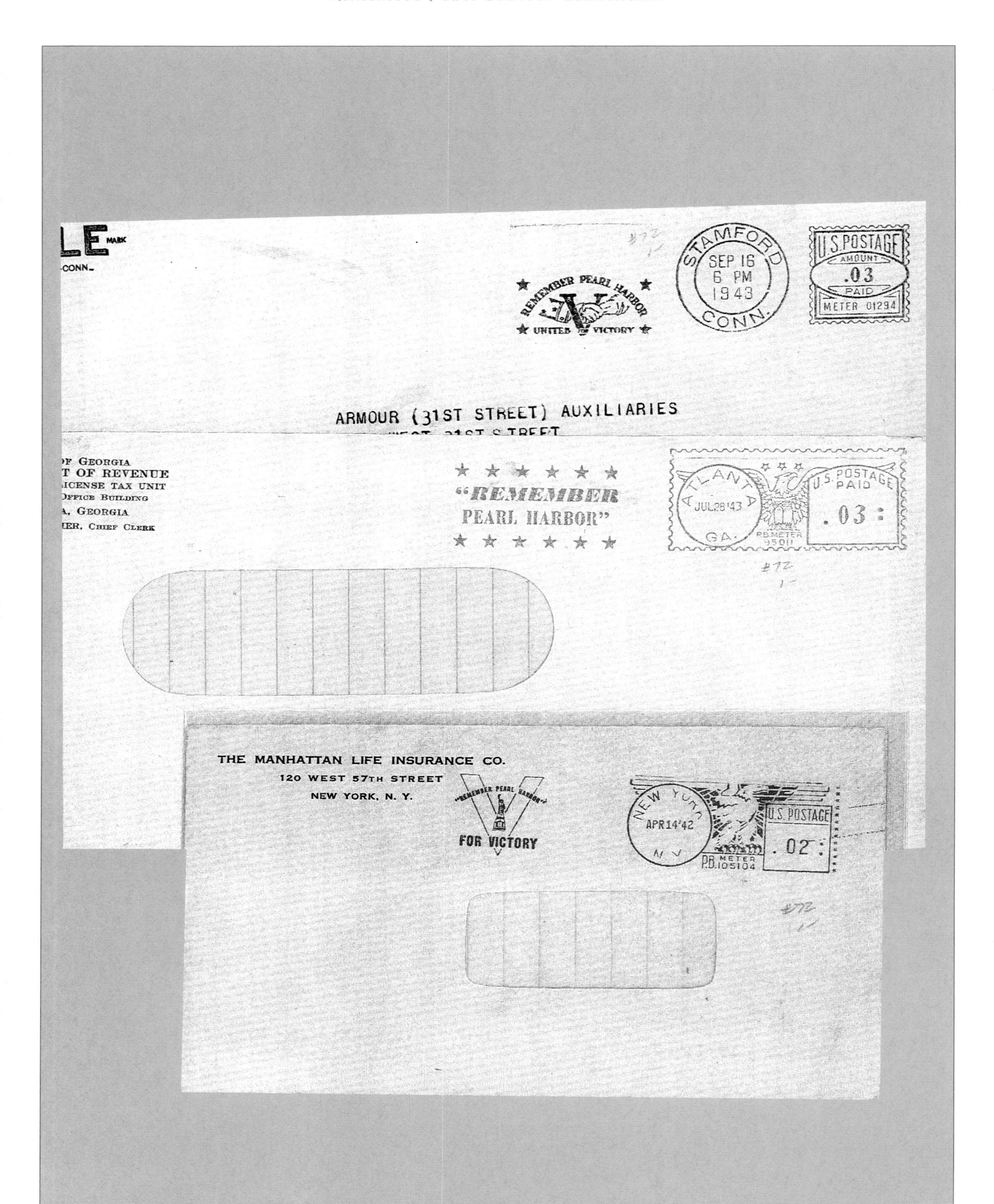
LE
CONN.
STAMFORD SEP 16 6 PM 1943 CONN.
U.S. POSTAGE AMOUNT .03 PAID METER 01294
REMEMBER PEARL HARBOR
UNITED FOR VICTORY
ARMOUR (31ST STREET) AUXILIARIES
OF GEORGIA
T OF REVENUE
LICENSE TAX UNIT
OFFICE BUILDING
A, GEORGIA
IER, CHIEF CLERK
"REMEMBER
PEARL HARBOR"
ATLANTA JUL 28 '43 GA.
U.S. POSTAGE PAID .03
THE MANHATTAN LIFE INSURANCE CO.
120 WEST 57TH STREET
NEW YORK, N. Y.
"REMEMBER PEARL HARBOR"
FOR VICTORY
NEW YORK APR 14 '42
U.S. POSTAGE .02
PB. METER 105104

Three-Dimensional Items

A

Ceramic bowl

B

Flag stand

Wood plaque

Chalkware doll

Statue

Bottle opener

Paper drinking cup

Chalkware cannon

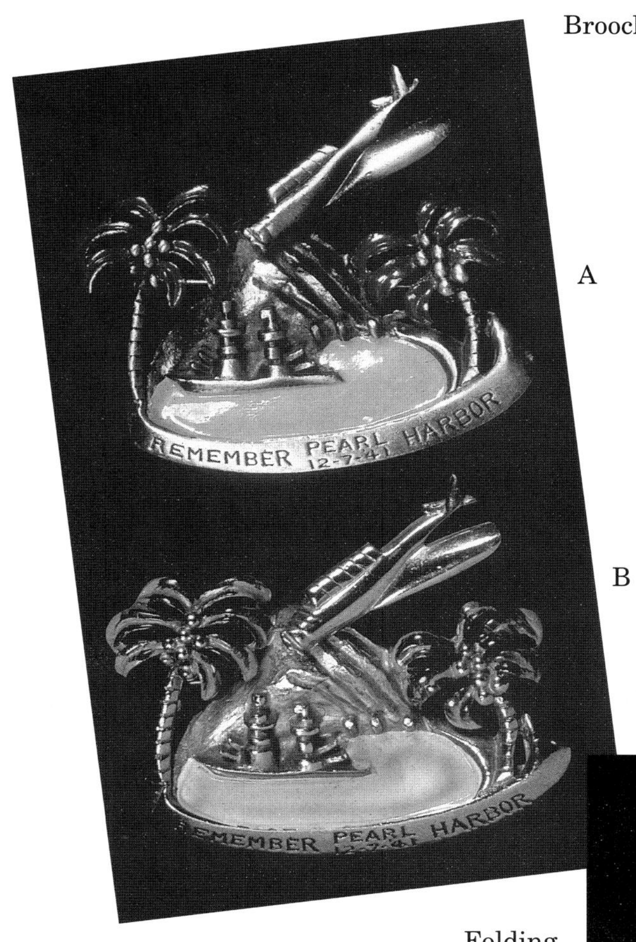

Brooches

Bottle

Folding knife

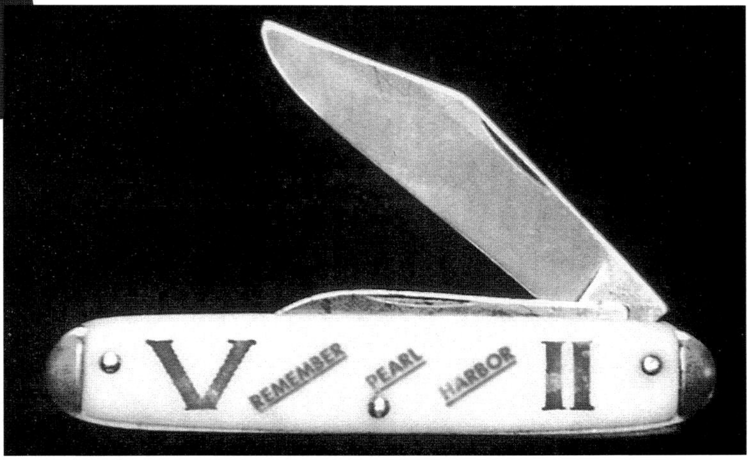

Fluorescent sign

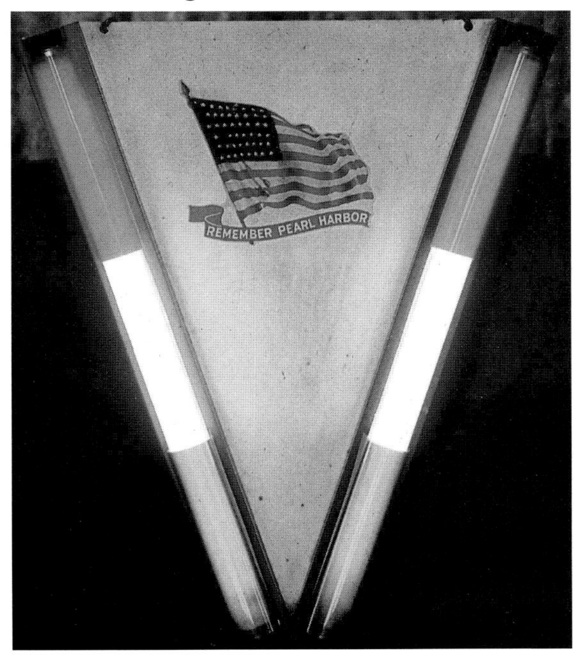

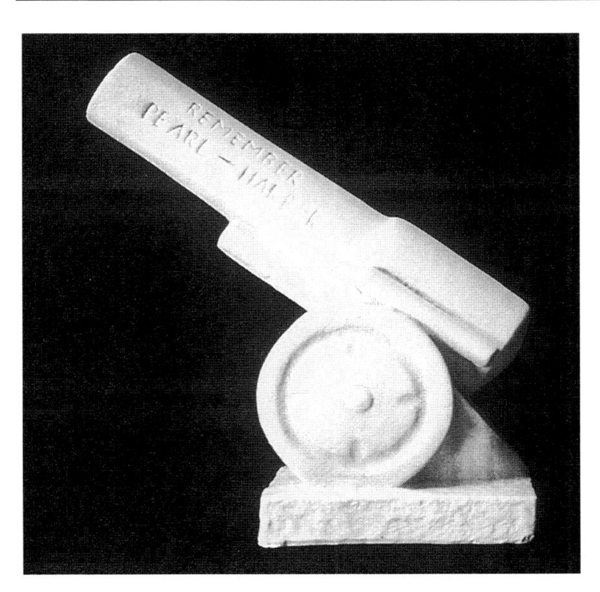

Chalkware cannon

Mechanical pencil

Bullet pencil

Puzzle

Milk glass trays

The foremast and the bridge of the USS *Arizona* collapsed forward to an eerie 45–degree angle when the forward section of the ship was destroyed by the magazine explosion. Three of her crew members would earn the Medal of Honor for their actions that day. USN

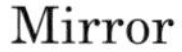
Mirror

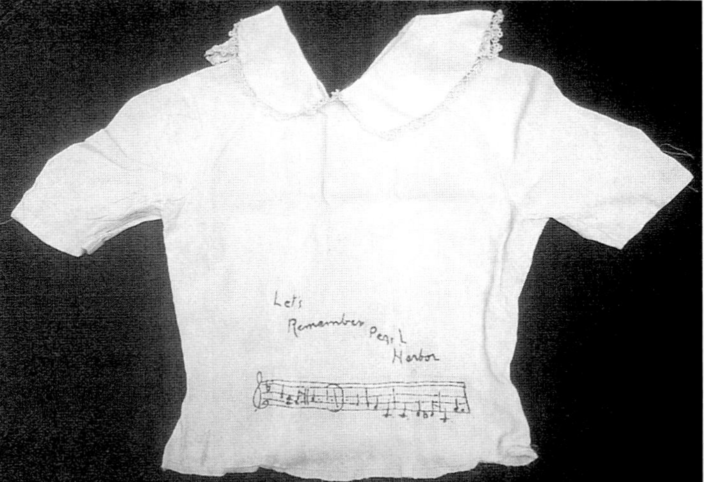

Patriotic blouse

Purse

Chalkware
showing USS *Arizona* on one side,
Remember Pearl Harbor on the other side.

Bank

Mechanical pencil

Lead pencil

The USS *Arizona*, *Tennessee* and *West Virginia*
burning on "battleship row." USN

Jewelry

Pendant

Assorted pins

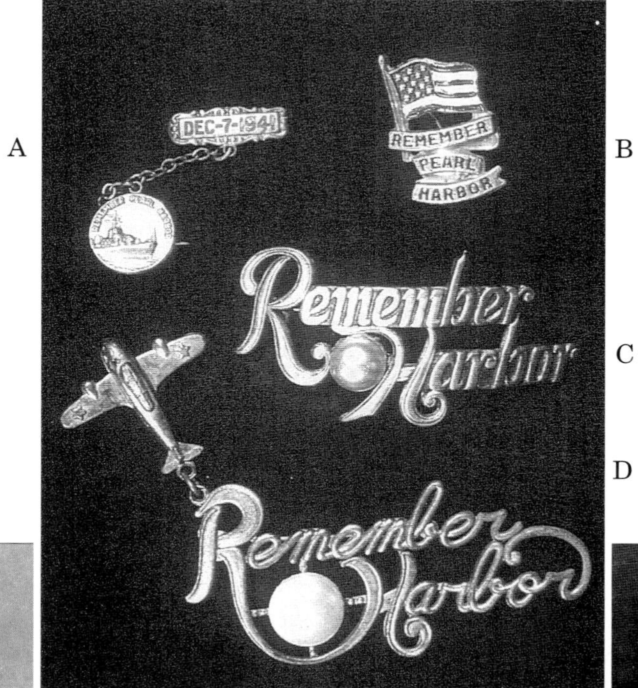

A

B

C

D

Looking over the wrecked aircraft at Hangar #6 on Ford Island. The destroyer *Shaw's* forward magazine has exploded sending a huge plume of fire and smoke skyward. USN

Badge

Pencil sharpener

Key fob

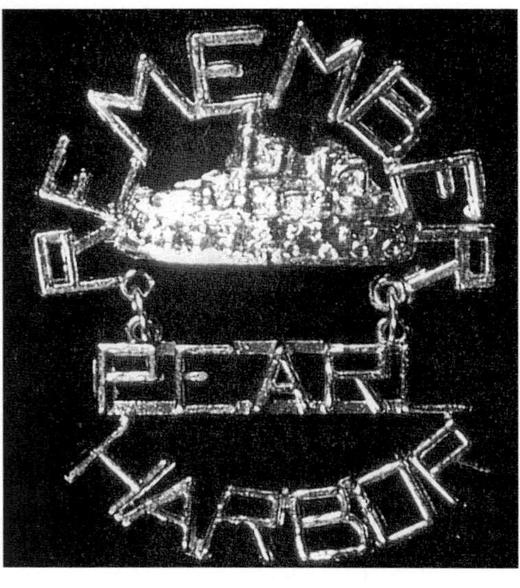

Pendant

Pins

A

B

Five air heroes of the Pearl Harbor attack who flew their P-36 and P-40 fighters against the Japanese invaders. From left to right: Lt. Harry W. Brown, 2nd Lt. Philip M. Rasmussen, 2nd Lt. Kenneth M. Taylor, 2nd Lt. George S. Welch, 1st Lt. Lewis M. Sanders. PHPC

Comic book cover and inside pages

This vicious anti-Japanese booklet was published in early 1941 by Street & Smith Publications, Inc. It is interesting reading for the intense propaganda message and the inaccuracies that were not known at the time.

1942 Pearl Harbor ticket for U.S. Navy Pearl Harbor Day War Bond Drive. This ticket was a $1.00 chance for a $1000 war bond. Ticket was originally for a $100 war bond, but was changed to $1000.

SPONSORED BY THE OKLAHOMA CITY STAMP CLUB

"THE EAGLE GROWS NEW PINIONS"
REMEMBER THE PANAY! REMEMBER THE ARIZONA!

Postal Covers

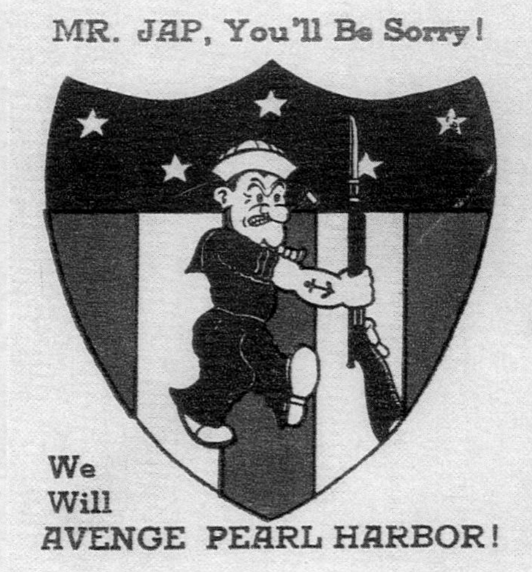

REMEMBER PEARL HARBOR!
COPYRIGHT BY
E. C. KROPP CO.
C135

Reveille
"REMEMBER PEARL HARBOR!"

Post cards

BOOM
BOOM
JUST A LITTLE
SOMETHING TO
"REMEMBER
PEARL HARBOR!"

Roosevelt Bust

Poster

Miniature Panties

GREETINGS
FROM
CHINATOWN
SAN FRANCISCO
DON'T GET
CAUGHT
WITH YOUR
PANTS DOWN!
REMEMBER
PEARL
HARBOR!

Pillow Cover

Matchbook

Banner

Assorted Pins

Punchboard

Poster

...we here highly resolve that these dead shall not have died in vain...

REMEMBER DEC. 7th!

Sticker

REMEMBER
PEARL
HARBOR

"Keep 'em Flying"

©1942 W. PELS
EVER READY LABEL CORP. N.Y.

Help the Boys in Service Exterminate These Rats—Buy War Bonds & Stamps!
©

Post card

Sticker

Plaque

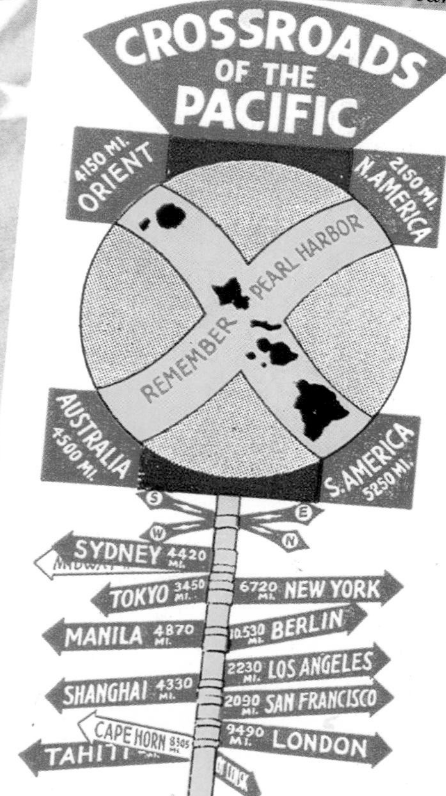

Post card

DRISCOLL, HONOLULU

Sticker

Sticker

Brooch

Pendant

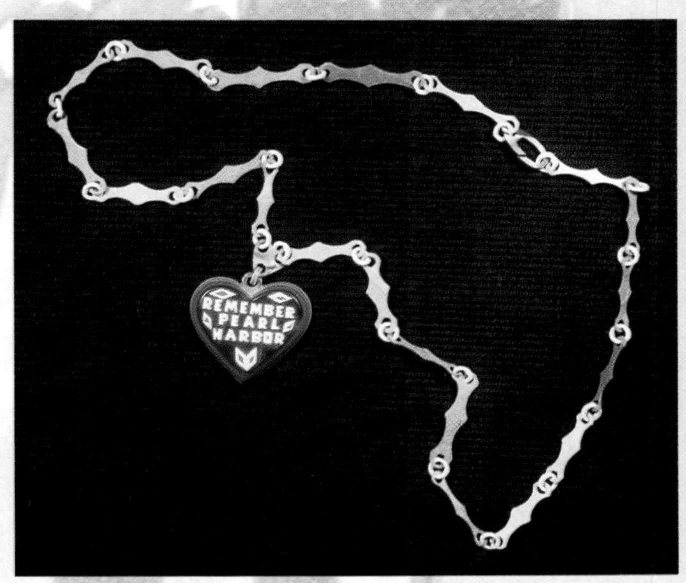

Pendant

Pendant

Brooch

Pendant

Badges

Pendant

Brooch

Pendant

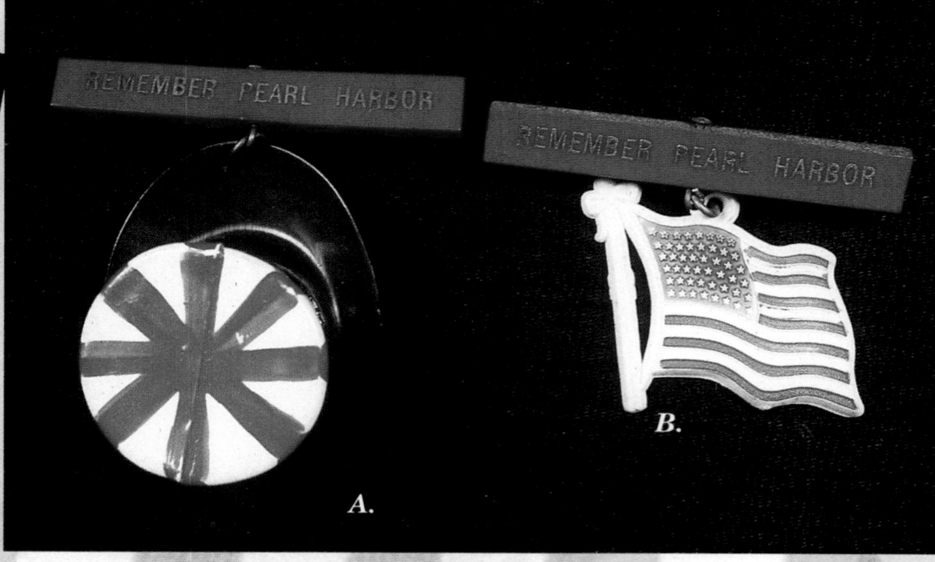

A.
B.

Scrapbook

Badge

License Plate with Topper

Calendar

Ribbon

Emblem

Paperweight

Cap

Scarf

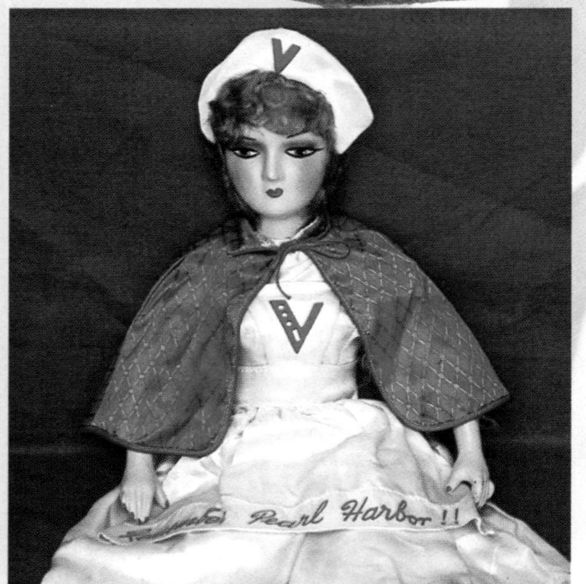
Bed Doll

Book

Cigar

License Reflector

Ribbon

Medallion

Badge

Chalkware

Badge

Sticker

Hat

Neckties

Banner

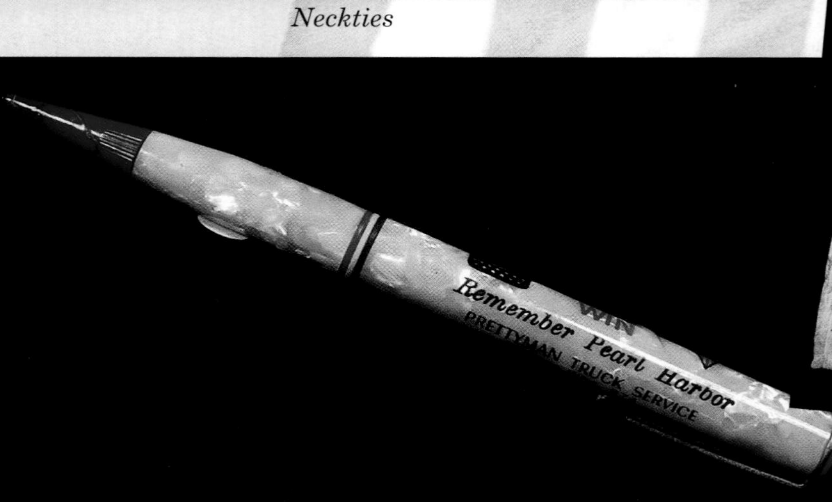

Mechanical Pen

Flag

Sticker

Handbag

Arcade Game

Sticker

Plaque

Pennant

Painting

Drinking Glass

Pillow Cover

Mirror

Magazine

Sticker

One of Hawaii's best known musicians and songwriters was Johnny Noble. He was long associated with the Moana and Royal Hawaiian hotels in Honolulu as a musician and director of entertainment. After the attack on Pearl Harbor, he wrote "Remember Pearl Harbor," which was not released until early 1942. A tune by the same name was written first by Don Reid with the tune composed by Reid and Sammy Kaye and released in late 1941.

Two different versions of the origin of this phrase have been around since the Pearl Harbor attack. The song was written and composed by Frank Loesser. The first version is that Chaplin Howell Forgy, serving on the USS *New Orleans* uttered these words while passing ammunition to a gun crew during the attack. The other is that Chaplin William A. McGuire who was on the USS *California* passed the communication during the attack. He later denied ever saying it.

Japan also remembered the attack on Pearl Harbor. On the first anniversary of the attack, the government issued a series of propaganda post cards. The aircraft carrier *Kaga*, present at Pearl Harbor, was sunk at the Battle of Midway in June, 1942.

Pin

Lapel pins

Brooch

Rows of P-36s and P-40s are parked undamaged at Wheeler Field during the initial phase of the attack. The untouched Schofield Barracks is in the foreground. "Gabby" Gabreski, later America's top living ace, received a citation for saving some of the aircraft by taxiing them to safety. He later got into the air after the attack. USN

Cartoon from the Office of War Information. Charles H. Alston, artist.

DORY MILLER

Miller was a mess attendant on the USS *West Virginia* at the time of the attack. He was recruited to man one of two idle machine guns on the signal bridge to help cover the men abandoning ship. In no time, Miller, a tall back man innocent of previous gunnery drill, was shooting away, wearing the first smile anyone could recall his having since his recent Pacific Fleet heavyweight boxing triumph. For years the story was that he shot down any number of Japanese aircraft, but in fact this was untrue. He was, however, regarded as the first of his race to be awarded the Navy Cross. Some accounts even placed Miller on board the USS *Arizona*. He was killed on Thanksgiving Day 1943 while on board the torpedoed aircraft carrier *Liscombe Bay*.

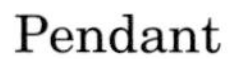
Pendant

A

B

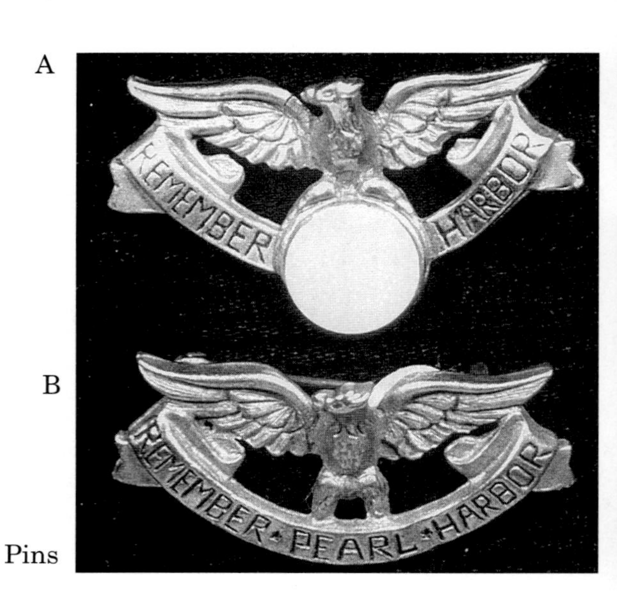

Pins

Badge

Badges

Pendant

Pin

Brooch

A B C

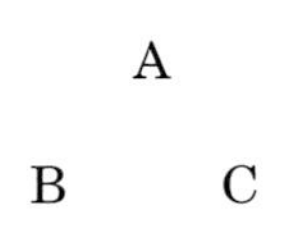

A

B C

Booklet

Book pages

Movies, Books & Magazines

While this book was published after the war, it was perhaps the first popular, factual history written about the attack. Walter Lord was with the OSS during the war and wrote many popular histories, including the *Battle of Midway, Sinking of the Titanic* and *The Battle of the Alamo.*

Program

OLD GLORY . . long may it wave!

Remember...

PEARL HARBOR

Englewood . . Kenwood-Hyde Park

JOINT PATRIOTIC MEETING

TUESDAY, FEBRUARY 3, 1942

Thomas E. Fleming President Englewood	Sylvester W. Cotter President Kenwood - Hyde Park
Milton Cruse Secretary Englewood	John J. McBride Secretary Kenwood - Hyde Park

This Republic Picture was made in early 1942, probably the first Hollywood propaganda film made after the attack. Hollywood heroics and cliches abound in the film which features Barry ducking out on his buddies, who are killed during the attack, and then he must redeem himself.

Plaques

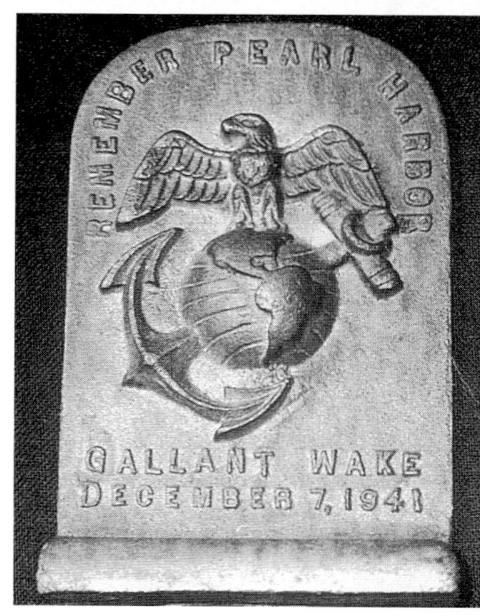

Bookend

Plaques & Plates

Plaque

Plaque

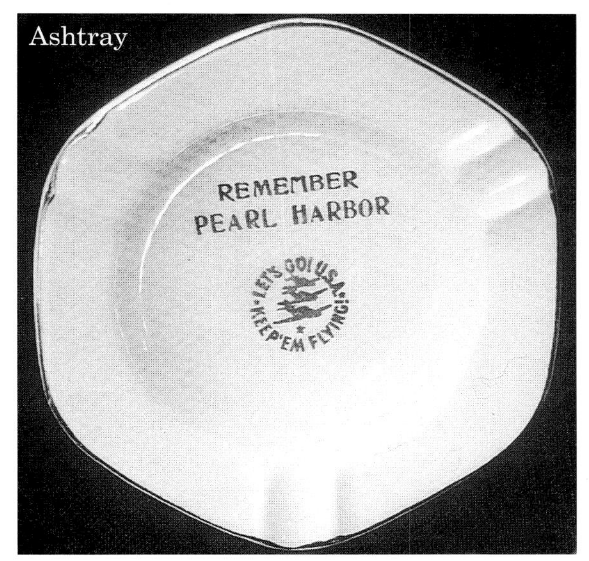

Ashtray

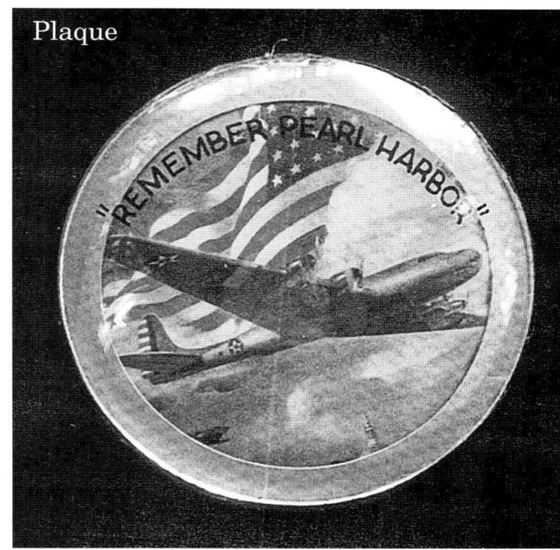

Plaque

Plaque

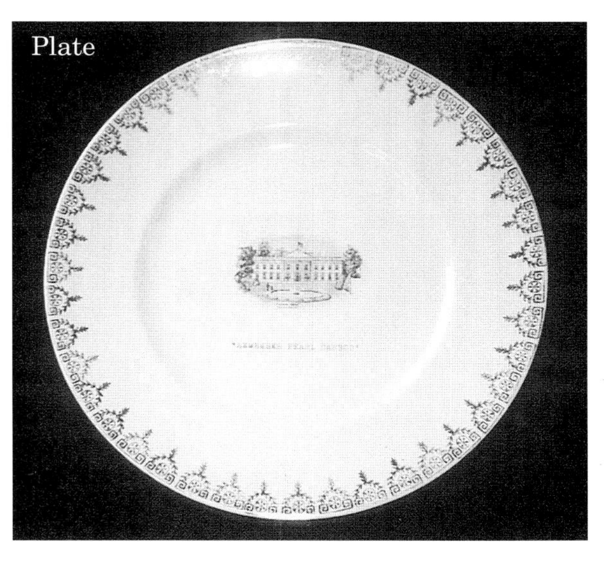
Plate

Desk plate

License plate

Greeting card and message inside

Ruler

Miscellaneous

Scarf

Handkerchief

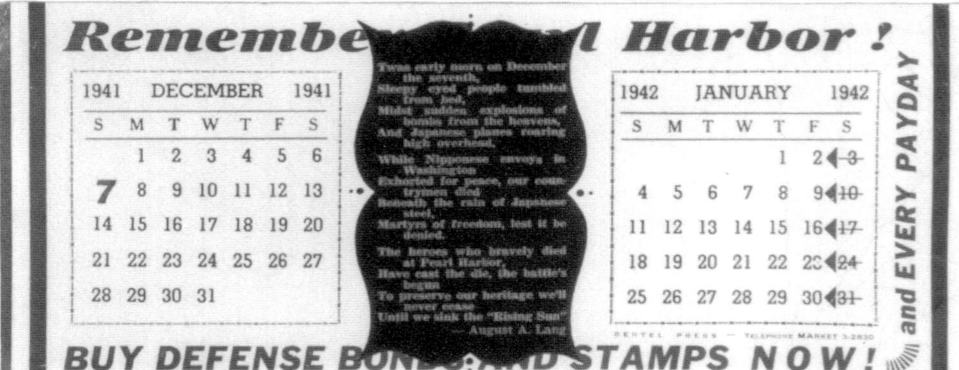

Blotter

Calendar

Lincoln pennies stamped "Remember Pearl Harbor" V Buy Defense Bonds V

Ribbon commemorating the launching of the submarine USS *Snook* at Portsmouth, New Hampshire.

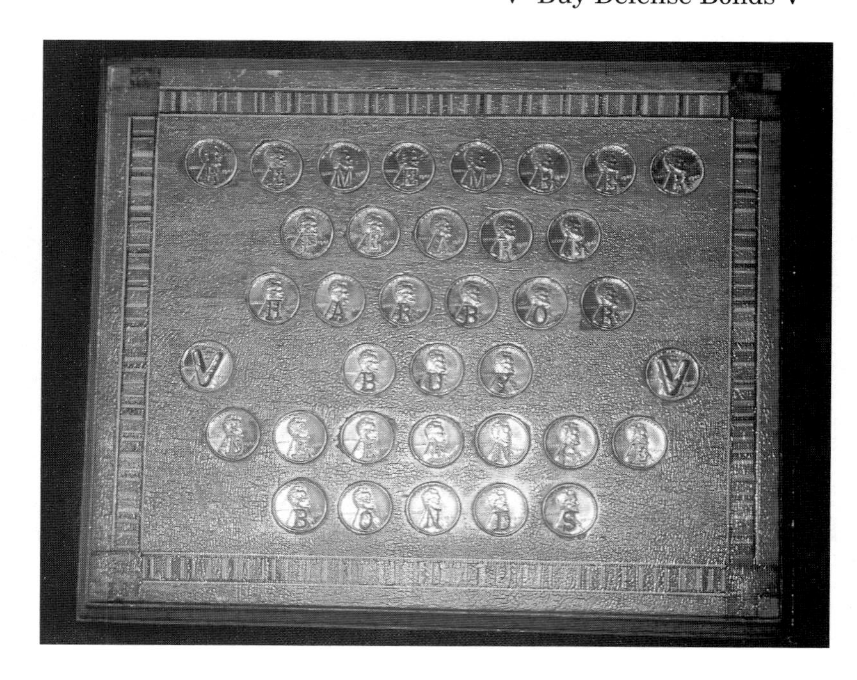

Handkerchief

Miniature panties.

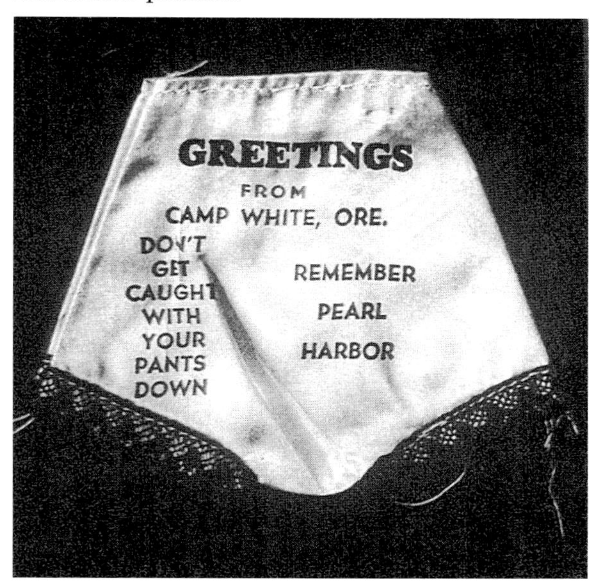

Flag boxes with flags.

REMEMBER PEARL HARBOR

Sixth Naval District

Charleston Navy Yard

War Bond Certificate

Awarded to

ELMER G. GRAY

This certificate is awarded for your voluntary participation in the NAVY PAYROLL SAVINGS PLAN and for purchasing an extra War Bond during the December 7 Navy War Bond Campaign. This expression of tribute is dedicated to the men of our Armed Forces all over the world who are sacrificing their lives so that the Freedoms of our people may be made secure.

JULES JAMES,
Rear Admiral, U. S. Navy
Commandant Sixth Naval District
and Navy Yard, S. C.

7 DECEMBER 1943

Mountain Sweets

Hand Decorated Sugars

BEREA COLLEGE STUDENT INDUSTRIES

Sugar Tablets with applied design containing sugar, egg albumen, and U. S. Certified color.
Hand Decorated and distributed by Berea College Student Industries Candy Kitchen, Berea, Kentucky.
Net Weight 3¼ oz.

Berea College students of Berea, Kentucky, hand–decorated sugar cubes with patriotic slogans to sell as their contribution to the war effort.

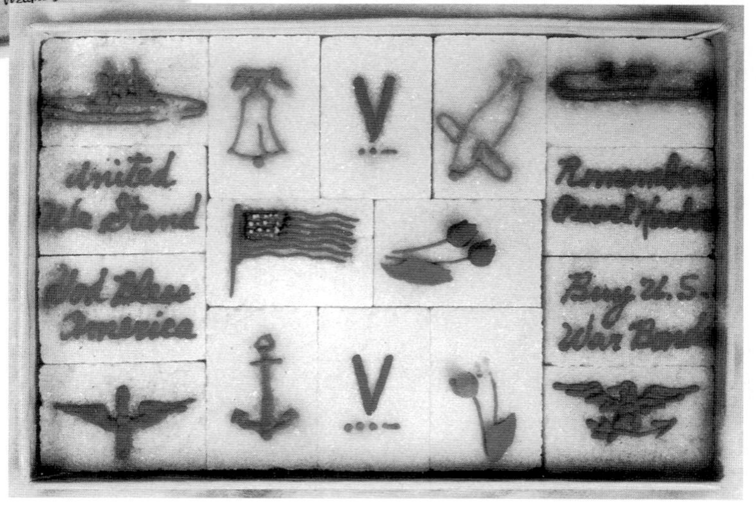

License plate attachments

License plate

License plate

KEEP EM FLYING V REMEMBER PEARL HARBOR

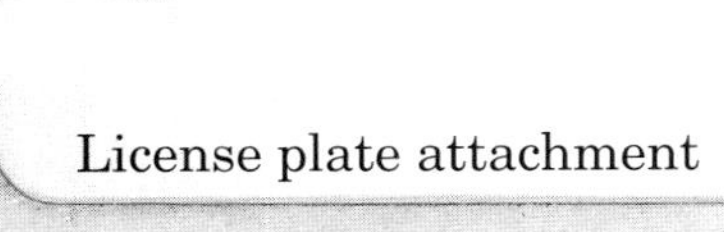

License plate attachment

REMEMBER PEARL HARBOR!

JAPANESE HUNTING LICENSE

Season Now Open — For the Duration
ISSUED: Dec. 7, 1941

FEE: Loyalty to American Ideals.
BOUNTY: Gratitude of 130,000,000 True Americans

This is to Certify That JOHN RAY SCOTT
IS ENTITLED TO HUNT THE JAPANESE RAT, and is hereby warned to exercise extreme caution in approaching this savage beast: it is a vicious animal and strikes from behind without warning.

This animal has the characteristics of a skunk in appearance and odor, but has an appetite for women and children instead of small fowls. Look for the yellow stripe down its back.

In shooting this stinkin' skunk, aim at its stomach, since it has lots of GUTS, but no heart or brains.

Issued by IRENE A. KUBIAK

Game Warden — *Uncle Sam*

Clerk — *Hari Kari*

REMEMBER PEARL HARBOR · KEEP 'EM DYING

This license expires soon, we hope.

Scarf

HAWAII INVASION CURRENCY

The threat of a Japanese invasion was considered a possibility in 1942, even after the decisive battle of Midway. By August the federal government had withdrawn all regular currency used in Hawaii and replaced it with specially printed notes. These had "Hawaii" overprinted in large letters on the back and vertically at each end on the front. The old money was burned in a sugar mill at Aiea, and after August 15, 1942, it became illegal to possess, without a license, the regular notes. The reasoning was that in the event of an invasion, the new notes would automatically become invalid, as they were restricted to Hawaii and the South Pacific area. They were free to circulate after October 1944 and were withdrawn by April 1946 when they were replaced with regular, old notes. The $1 notes were overprinted on series 1935A Silver Certificates. The $5, $10 and $20 notes were overprinted on Federal Reserve notes of the 12th (San Francisco) District 5. Five dollar and $20 notes were also overprinted on series 1934 and 1934A certificates, and the $10 note only on the 1934A certificate. All notes were printed on sheets of 12.

USS *California,* listing to port and smoking profusely at about 1000 hours as men in the foreground are watching from Ford Island headquarters building for hostile planes. The order to abandon ship has already been given as drifting fuel oil from the *Arizona* and *West Virginia* burns on the water. By the evening of December 9, the *California* will sink on an even keel and settle on the bottom. Her watertight integrity was lessened because of an impending hull inspection that required many of her hatches and manhole covers to be open for thorough venting of tanks and voids. NA

Pillow cover

Flag

Pillow cover

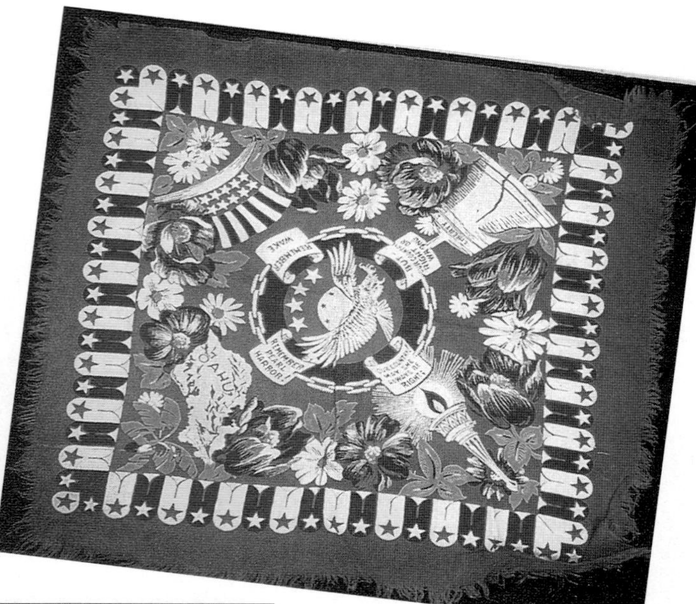

Scarf

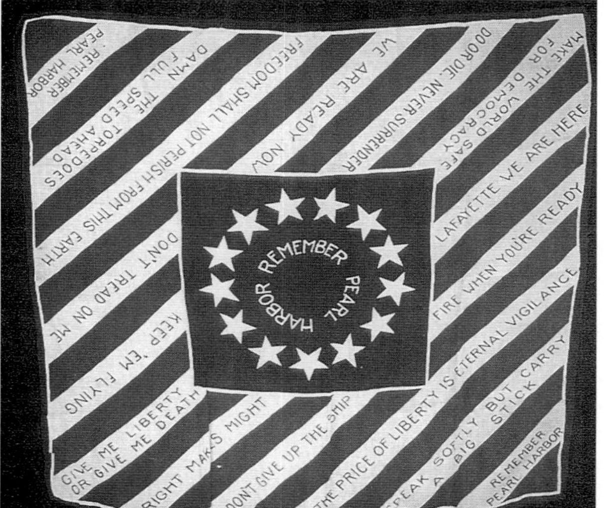

Handkerchiefs

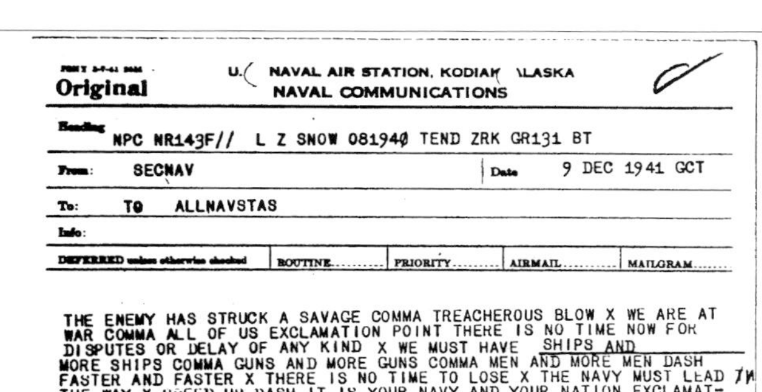

U.S. NAVAL AIR STATION, KODIAK ALASKA
NAVAL COMMUNICATIONS

Original

Heading: NPC NR143F// L Z SNOW 081940 TEND ZRK GR131 BT

From: SECNAV | Date: 9 DEC 1941 GCT

To: TO ALLNAVSTAS

Info:

DEFERRED unless otherwise checked | ROUTINE | PRIORITY | AIRMAIL | MAILGRAM

THE ENEMY HAS STRUCK A SAVAGE COMMA TREACHEROUS BLOW X WE ARE AT WAR COMMA ALL OF US EXCLAMATION POINT THERE IS NO TIME NOW FOR DISPUTES OR DELAY OF ANY KIND X WE MUST HAVE SHIPS AND MORE SHIPS COMMA GUNS AND MORE GUNS COMMA MEN AND MORE MEN DASH FASTER AND FASTER X THERE IS NO TIME TO LOSE X THE NAVY MUST LEAD THE WAY X SPEED UP DASH IT IS YOUR NAVY AND YOUR NATION EXCLAMATION POINT SIGNED FRANK KNOX SECRETARY OF THE NAVY X PARAGRAPH X NAVAL ACRIVITIES WILL POST ON ALL BULLETIN BOARDS INSPECTORS WILL REQUEST MAXIMUM PUBLICITY BY NAVAL CONTRACTORS X ALL SUGGESTIONS FOR THE REMOVAL OF RESTRICTIONS OF EVERY NATURE WHICH WILL ELIMINATE OR TEND TO ELIMINATE DELAY IN PRODUCTION WILL BE WELCOME.

09035 1705 HB ON 58 KCS.

A–Denotes action I–Denotes information X–Denotes copy only

Telegram

Magazine ad

Pay-off for Pearl Harbor!

Three years ago, the sneak attack on Pearl Harbor found America unprepared to defend its rights. Yet, even at that early date, Cadillac was in its third year of building aircraft engine parts for military use. Today we look hopefully forward to the time when this important contribution to America's air power will pay off in such a scene as that illustrated above.

For more than five years we have been working toward that end. Back in 1939, we started building precision parts for Allison—America's famous liquid-cooled aircraft engine—used to power such potent fighters as the Lightning, the Warhawk, the Mustang, the Airacobra and the new Kingcobra.

In addition to our work for Allison, which has included more than 57,000,000 man-hours of precision production—we assisted Army Ordnance Engineers in designing the M-5 Light Tank and the M-8 Howitzer motor carriage, and have produced them in quantities. Both are powered by Cadillac engines, equipped with Hydra-Matic transmissions.

We are now building other weapons which utilize some of our Cadillac peacetime products. We can't talk about all of them yet—but we are confident they will prove significant additions to Allied armor.

CADILLAC MOTOR CAR DIVISION GENERAL MOTORS CORPORATION

LET'S ALL
BACK THE ATTACK
BUY WAR BONDS

War bond holder

REMEMBER PEARL HARBOR!!

WAR
BUY ~~DEFENSE~~ BONDS
AND KEEP 'EM FLYING

PROPERTY OF

PROTECT your Defense Bonds. Even though the bonds are registered you will want to safeguard them. We suggest that you store your bonds in a safe deposit box at this bank, where they will have the protection of our strong vault. The cost is very little; the peace of mind is great.

WAR ~~DEFENSE~~ BONDS
ARE IDEAL ANNIVERSARY AND BIRTHDAY GIFTS

Play money

10
PAY TO THE BEARER
TEN DOLLARS IN FUN
Remember Pearl Harbor
Keep 'em Flying
"THAT GOVERNMENT OF THE PEOPLE
BY THE PEOPLE AND FOR THE PEOPLE
SHALL NOT PERISH FROM THE EARTH"
10
10
10

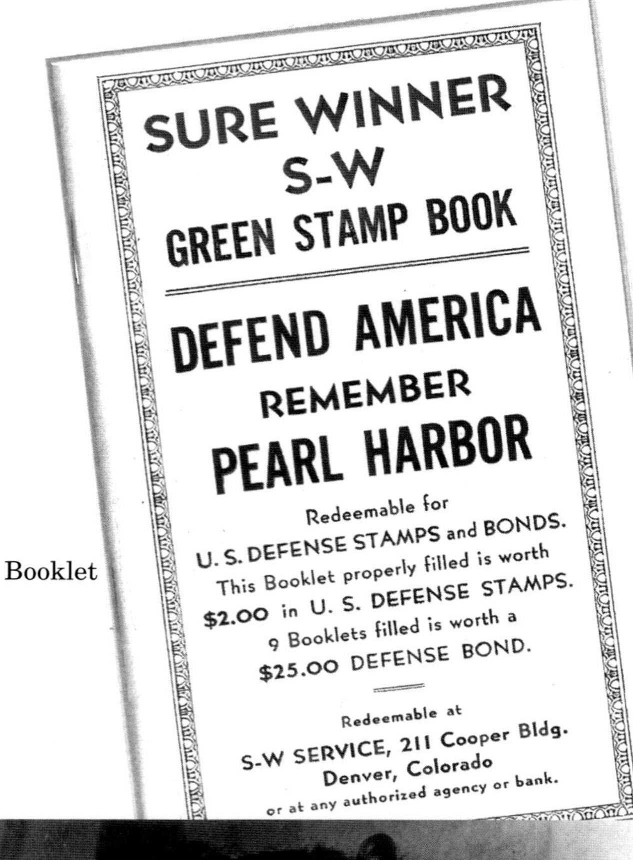

Booklet

WARNING

THIS CRIMINAL is Heavily Armed and Dangerous At All Times. He Prefers Treacherous Sneak Attacks and Specializes in Murdering Unarmed Civilians. He Secures His Information Thru the Careless Talk of His Victims.

EVERY PERSON and EVERY DOLLAR IS NEEDED FOR THE ELIMINATION OF THIS FIEND.

REWARD

For the Capture of this Murderous Lunatic the Reward is

FREEDOM , SECURITY

PEACE

ONATED BY

AMES F ANDERSON USN RET USS SC

COMPLIMENTS OF MERCANTILE PRINTING CO., LTD.
10, to 14 MERCHANT STREET HONOLULU

Circular

Miss Myrtle Bergheim, White House secretary, holds a check for $70,000 written on a wood and metal wing flap of a Japanese airplane shot down during the Pearl Harbor attack. The workers at the Pearl Harbor Navy Yard, instead of accepting their wages for working on Labor Day, sent them to the President in the form of this unique check, which was turned over to the U.S. Treasury. FDR

Cincpac File
Pac-08- wlw
P15/P

Serial 1[illegible]2

APR 27 1943

UNITED STATES PACIFIC FLEET
FLAGSHIP OF THE COMMANDER IN CHIEF

From: Commander in Chief, United States Pacific Fleet.
To: Granvil Ray Williams, 360-10-06, GM3c, USN.

Via: Commanding Officer, U.S.S. WEST VIRGINIA.

Subject: Purple Heart - award of.

Enclosure: (A) Purple Heart Ribbon.

1. In the name of the President and by direction of the Secretary of the Navy the Purple Heart is awarded by the Commander in Chief, United States Pacific Fleet to:

GRANVIL RAY WILLIAMS, GM3c, UNITED STATES NAVY

for wounds received in action against an organized enemy, during the attack on Pearl Harbor, T.H., on December 7, 1941.

C. W. Nimitz

C. W. NIMITZ

August 1943

Copy to:
SecNav
BuPers
Personnel Jacket

Pearl Harbor Survivor GM2C Granvil R. Williams in August 1943, his Navy jumper and sailor cap and his Purple Heart Award for wounds received December 7th.

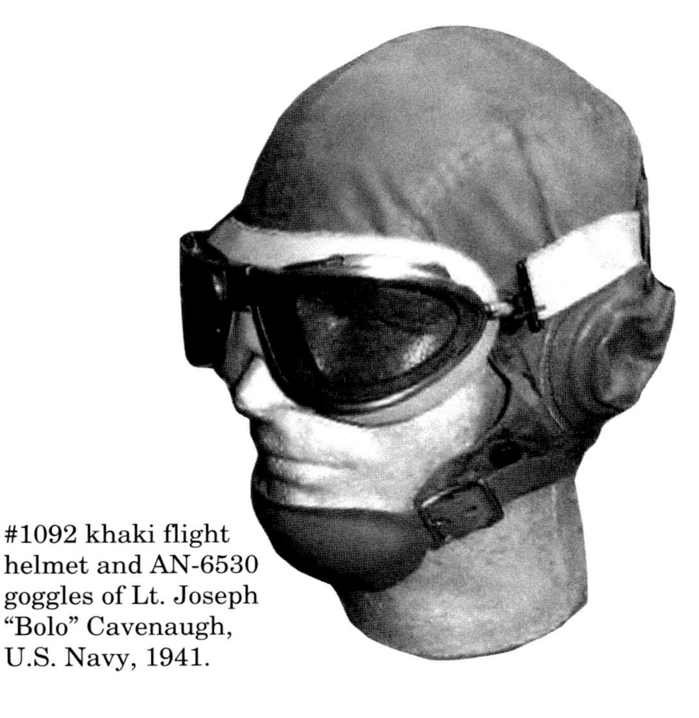

#1092 khaki flight helmet and AN-6530 goggles of Lt. Joseph "Bolo" Cavenaugh, U.S. Navy, 1941.

Japanese aviator leather flight helmet and goggles, circa 1941.

Pearl Harbor Remembers

USCGC TANEY MEMORIAL
When the Japanese attack on Pearl Harbor began on 7 December 1941, the Coast Guard Cutter TANEY was moored at Pier 6 in downtown Honolulu. She was one of the first U.S. ships to offer naval gunfire support and successfully defended Honolulu's primary power plant from enemy aircraft. During the war the TANEY saw action in the Atlantic and Pacific oceans and in the Mediterranean Sea. After a retrofit in 1944, the TANEY became the flagship for the Okinawa Campaign, serving as command and control center and shooting down two kamikaze attacks and an explosive-laden seaplane.

Near the Aloha Tower, downtown Honolulu.

Fort Shafter

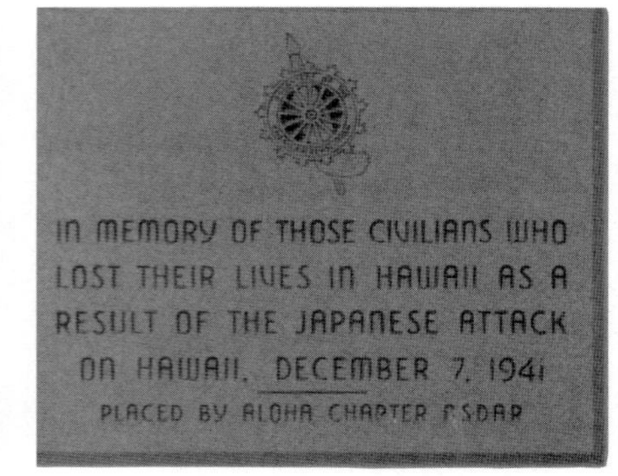

On the front of the Hawaii State Library.

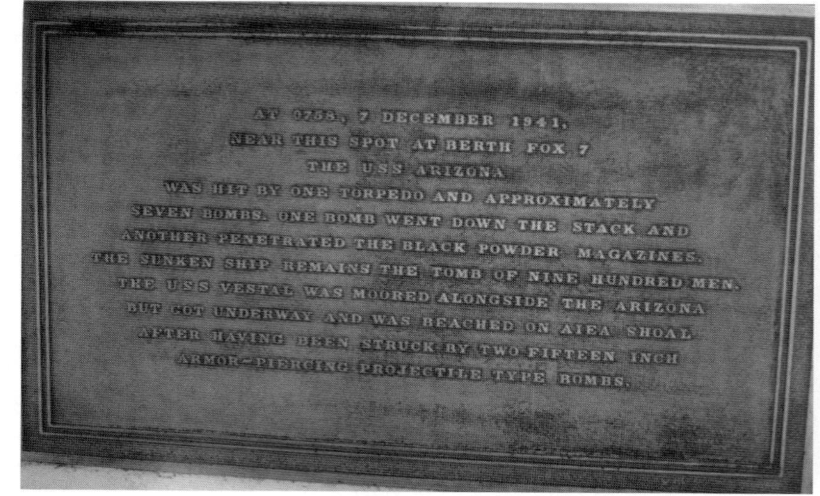

USS *Arizona* plaque on Ford Island.

The *Arizona* rock on Ford Island, placed by the Navy Club of the United States of America, December 7, 1955.

Summary of the Pearl Harbor Attack

U.S. Personnel Casualties:

	Killed	Wounded	Total
Navy	1,998	710	2,708
Army	233	364	597
Marines	109	69	178
Civilians	68	35	103
Total	2,408	1,178	3,586

Aircraft Damage

	Lost	Damaged
U.S. Navy	92	31
Army Air Corps	77	128
Total	169	159

U.S. Ships Damaged or Sunk (*)

- * *Arizona*
- * *California*
- *Maryland*
- *Nevada*
- * *Oklahoma*
- *Pennsylvania*
- *Tennessee*
- * *West Virginia*
- *Helena*
- *Honolulu*
- *Raleigh*
- *Cassin*
- *Downes*
- *Helm*
- *Shaw*
- *Oglala*
- *Curtiss (AV-4)*
- * *Sotoyomo (YT-9)*
- * *Utah (AG-16)*
- *Vestal (AR-4)*
- * *YFD-2*

U.S. Ships Present at Pearl Harbor (or within 3 miles of Oahu)

Battleships	8	Yard Oilers	5
Heavy Cruisers	2	Water Barges	3
Light Cruisers	6	Torpedo Test Barge	1
Destroyers	30	Chinese Junk	1
Minecraft	23	Dredge	1
Misc. Aux.	3	Repair (AR)	3
Net Vessels	6	Oilers	2
PT Boats	12	Ammunition	1
Yard Patrol	1	Fleet Tugs	3
Floating Dry Dock	1	Yard Tugs	9
Seaplane Derricks	4	Garbage Lighters	3
Submarines	4	Repair Barges	3
Tender (AD)	2	U.S. Coast Guard	6
Tender (AV)	6	Pile Driver	1
Tender (AS)	1	Misc. Yard Craft	19
Sub. Rescue	1	Ferryboats	2
Gunboat	1	Stores	3
Hospital	1		
		Total	**178**

Firing volleys over bodies of 15 officers and men who perished in the attack on the Kaneoka Naval Air Station December 7. USN

Authors

Frank B. Arian was born in Los Angeles, California about the time of the Cuban Missile Crisis; his father Jack is the owner of a large chain of Army surplus stores called The Supply Sergeant. Frank grew up in the surplus business, and some of his earliest memories relate to Army surplus. He remembers climbing on a mountain of jungle boots his father purchased as a wholesale lot from the government just after the Tet Offensive of 1968. He also recalls vividly a tour through a factory that was producing spools of concertina wire destined for the southeast Asian theater. Over the years Frank developed expertise in authentic uniforms and field gear and in edged weapons. In particular, he is knowledgeable about tiger stripe uniforms of the Vietnam war, including the many in–country variants, and in Rhodesian camouflage. His expertise became well known to the numerous movie studios in the Los Angeles area, which afforded him the opportunity to outfit many film productions, including *The Deer Hunter, Uncommon Valor,* and *Terminator 2,* among others.

While at the University of California, Santa Cruz, in the late 1970s, Frank became involved with predatory birds. As a field research associate with the Santa Cruz Predatory Bird Research Group, he spent thousands of hours in the field documenting Peregrine falcon behavior in an attempt to reintroduce the species to their former ranges. He also worked on the Philippines Monkey–Eating Eagle project in Mindanao, Philippines. In addition, Frank has become increasing involved with back–country medicine and has completed the Red Cross Advanced First Aid–Mountaineering instructor course and an Emergency Medical Technician course.

Frank returned to University of California, Davis, in 1986 to complete his Bachelors degree in Biological Sciences. He subsequently was accepted to and graduated from Case Western Reserve University School of Medicine in Cleveland with an M.D. in 1996. Following graduation, he completed three years of an Emergency Medicine residency at Kern County Medical Center in Bakersfield, California. He currently resides there with his golden retriever and practices at local urgent care facilities.

Since leaving his residency, Frank has had much time to devote to his true passion, studying and collecting WWII home front items. After contributing to Martin Jacobs' price guide to home front collectibles, Frank founded a major cyber–museum for home front memorabilia at:

www.ww2homefront.com

This website features photo archives of thousands of collectibles as well as stimulating didactics pertaining to this unique period of modern history. Other major projects include an Army surplus store/home front museum slated to open November 2000 in Bakersfield, and collaboration on three additional home front books, one of which is nearing completion. He writes, "Martin and I felt it was an ideal time to uncover finally those elusive 'Remember Pearl Harbor' collectibles that are so sought after by home front collectors. These collectibles have a large following, are distinctly American, and are feverishly patriotic. It is through these collectibles and the stories of Pearl Harbor survivors and their families that the resounding battle cry 'Remember Pearl Harbor' lives on."

Dr. Arian encourages all contact and can be reached by e-mail at one of two addresses:

drpackrat@webtv.net
packratdoc@aol.com

or by U.S. mail to:

Frank B. Arian, M.D.
P.O. Box 21478
Bakersfield, California 93390

or at his website:

www.ww2homefront.com.

Authors

Martin S. Jacobs was born in 1943 and is considered a "war baby." As an avid collector of Pearl Harbor mementos for the past 20 years, he claims it was his first collectible, a mechanical pencil inscribed with the ominous saying, "Let Us Not Forget Pearl Harbor" that was instrumental in beginning his vast collection, which he cherishes today. Though, it was a rendezvous at Pearl Harbor on an autumn Sunday in 1996 when Martin piloted a WWII AT–6 Texan over the USS Arizona Memorial, when rueful memories of sailors unaware of the unprovoked attack by the Japanese and the sailors' acts of heroism against their aggressors, that Martin decided to preserve their legacy by authoring this keepsake collectible book.

Today, Martin travels extensively to military and collectible shows, always looking for that special Pearl Harbor collectible to add to his collection. As a free-lance writer, he's had feature stories on the WWII home front published in national magazines and newspapers including *Stars and Stripes, Army and Navy News, Leatherneck, Veterans Press, Military Trader, Antique Trader, Collectors Eye, Toy Trader, Reminisce, Today's Collector, Collectit* and others. He was a major contributor to the WWII pictorials *To Win the War* and *For The Boys.*

In March of 2000, he authored his first collectibles book *World War II Homefront Collectibles—Price & Identification Guide*, the only book of its kind.

Martin would like to hear from his readers and offers free estimates on Pearl Harbor and related home-front collectibles and memorabilia. He may be reached by e-mail or phone:

Mjacobs784@aol.com

Ph. (415) 661-7552

To order a copy of *World War II Homefront Collectibles—Price & Identification Guide,* send $22.95 plus $3.20 Priority Mail to:

Martin Jacobs
P.O. Box 22026
San Francisco CA 94122

Contributors

John Egger, Fair Haven, New Jersey, was born and raised in Baltimore, Maryland. Upon graduating from high school he enlisted in the U.S. Marine Corps, serving a tour of duty in Vietnam. He has been a police officer for over 20 years with both the Baltimore City Police Dept. as a Detective in the Homicide Squad and the New Jersey Transit Police as a training officer and instructor at several New Jersey police academies. John began collecting war souvenirs as a child in the 1950s and later began to focus his collection on World War II Japanese military headgear, uniforms and insignias. He has maintained an interest in the Pearl Harbor attack and started collecting "Remember Pearl Harbor" items in the late 1980s. John was instrumental in the production of this book, assisting with photographs from his collection.

Larry Shedwick, Ford City, Pennsylvania, is a retired Biology/Life Science teacher of 33 years in Pittsburgh and Ford City. While in grade school during the war, Larry began collecting when he found a "Remember Pearl Harbor" window decal just like the one his grandfather had on his front door. Today, Larry and his wife Kay present displays and give seminars on the World War II home front and sweetheart jewelry around the country. Some of Larry's most sentimental "Remember Pearl Harbor" collectibles are pictured in this book.

Also special thanks to **Ken Fleck** and **Jim Lowe** for their assistance in the book.

Victory

We have remembered Pearl Harbor for 60 years. We will not forget it tomorrow. We must not forget those who sacrificed, but we must also remember the reason for their sacrifice. They died to create a better world for those of us who followed them. Their sacrifice was not in vain.

It is a distinct honor that we present to you the *Remember Pearl Harbor Collectibles* book, which brings you the greatest accumulation of collectibles and memorabilia compiled into one volume.

The Authors

V–J Day on Market Street in San Francisco, California. Photo by Gabrial Moulin. The stigma of Pearl Harbor had been lifted.

V–J in Honolulu. The attack on Pearl Harbor had been avenged.
HA

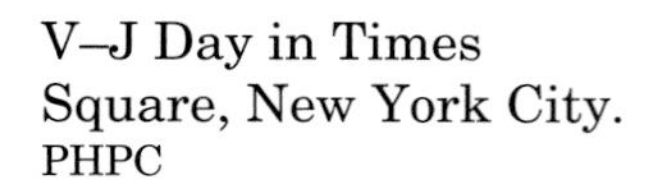

V–J Day in Times Square, New York City.
PHPC